THE MUSHROOM COOKBOOK

THE MUSHROOM COOKBOOK

A guide to edible wild and cultivated mushrooms ...
... and delicious seasonal recipes to cook with them

Michael Hyams and Liz O'Keefe

LORENZ BOOKS

CONTENTS

INTRODUCTION

Welcome to the world of mushrooms. Festivals are held for them, national holidays exist in their honour and their mystique has permeated art and literature for centuries. A rich source of nutrition, as well as being incredibly tasty of course, mushrooms are an amazing source of sustainable food that's also friendly to the environment along the way. Fat-, cholesterol-, and gluten-free and very low in sodium content, mushrooms even help us fight heart disease and HIV, and support the nervous system. Folklore, herbalists and Chinese medicine have all treasured mushrooms for their healing properties. Be assured, mushrooms are powerful things and they are everywhere.

Coming in many different forms and guises, mushrooms can taste wood-like, nutty and even of fruit, and can emulate the looks of eggs, fish, coral and vegetation depending on what type they are – eluding and confusing taxonomists along the way. They survive, evolve and are natural decomposers, mostly bringing balance to their natural surroundings and efficiency within a controlled-farming environment.

Neither fruit nor vegetable, mushrooms are spongy, fleshy, porous, and fruity parts of a larger fungus body – and are one of the most fantastic natural occurrences. Currently, the largest living organism on earth is thought to be a 3.8km (2½mile) honey fungus in Oregon, existing, sadly, under the soil where no one can see it. And while we are on startling mushroom facts, there are more than 2,300 species of edible and medicinal fungi available. Now that's a few books' worth…

Individual mushrooms in the wild rely on different weather conditions, surroundings and temperatures to thrive, but one thing that joins them, quite literally, is that they sprout up from a hidden world underground, with some types of mushroom living off and entwining with tree roots in a mutually beneficial arrangement, known scientifically as mycorrhiza. The mushroom co-exists with tree roots, making its own little (or rather large) mushroom city, taking in much-needed oxygen and carbohydrates from the tree to then produce the fruit we call 'mushrooms' above ground. Other mushrooms, which fall under the saprotroph category, feed off nutrition in the soil and dead matter, again connected by a larger mushroom body below the surface. Mushroom spores can be hidden – sometimes they have the right conditions they need to grow and sometimes they are taken over by another more dominating mushroom spore, and won't grow again the next year.

Mousserons >

Even though this book covers only 30 or so of the culinary mushrooms we eat in restaurants and at home today, it is fascinating to realise the extent of how mushrooms affect our lives. They are indeed everywhere. Mushrooms are so much more than a food commodity tucked in with the vegetables at the supermarket – when it comes to the forests, earth, construction and medicine, they are a powerhouse, literally holding us together. Fungi are behind fundamental new medicines, materials and energy production, as well as being hidden away in all kinds of foods. Fungi are the blue veins in blue cheese, are responsible for the fizz in your drinks and even make up some of the protein in pet food.

But you don't have to be a scientist to use mushrooms in the kitchen. Our book touches on the differences between mycorrhizal, parasitic and saprotrophic mushrooms, but this volume is really for mushroom cooks who are excited by the culinary possibilities of the ever-growing range of wild and cultivated mushrooms becoming available. Used in some of the most inventive cuisines, mushrooms are our passion, and we hope to pass that on to you. The Mushroom Cookbook can be dipped into wherever you please – you can start by cooking a certain mushroom in a recipe and look up information on it in the directory if you like it or start by devouring the profiles to find which mushroom you fancy experimenting with first. Let the journey begin!

Michael Hyams and Liz O'Keefe

Important note: this book is a guide to the wonderful range of mushrooms available to buy and how to cook with them, and not an identification guide for foraging. Many mushrooms can look similar in the field but are not all safe to eat, and the advice is to only obtain mushrooms from a trustworthy source. Some species of mushroom can cause allergic reactions in a few people.

WHAT IS A MUSHROOM?

The mushroom world is vast and intricate, and there are many terms to consider, like divisions, classes, families and genus. Some mushrooms share the same division and class, whereas some won't have anything in common with its neighbour in the forest or grass at all, though they all come under the one big fungus family tree.

The definition of 'fungus' (fungi in the plural) is an aerobic organism that lives by decomposing and absorbing organic material. Mycelium is the vegetative part of a fungus, a mass of probing, branch-like hyphae that act like threads growing throughout the soil or substrate. Mycelium generates from spores, and when two mycelium strains (mycelia) meet they can reproduce, producing fruiting bodies or what we like to call mushrooms.

As you'll see in the chart opposite, the different categories the mushrooms are placed in makes it easier for us to identify their similarities and what else they might have in common. It can also help in cooking. If you get your hands on some rare and expensive matsutake (part of the Tricholomataceae family), you can see from the chart that pied bleu is of the same family, and has similar characteristics like white chalky caps, thick stems and gills, and so can be cooked and prepared in the same way. The same goes for the oyster and eryngii, which are the same genus (Pleurotus), and when you start to examine them, you can see that they are virtually the same mushroom.

There are three main types of fungi, though the edible mushrooms are mostly mycorrhizal or saprotrophic. Mycorrhizal mushrooms grow in unison, entwining themselves amongst the tree roots from which they share nutrients and, most importantly, carbohydrates through the plant's ability to photosynthesize. There is also evidence that mycorrhizal mushrooms benefit the soil chemistry, with mycorrhizal soil being less prone to disease and drought. The fruits of mycorrhizal mushrooms will usually pop up around the base of a tree or where the roots travel around a forest, like the trompettes, girolles and morels.

Saprotrophic mushrooms grow on dying or dead wood; their spores are transferred airborne from other saprotrophic mushrooms. They are natural composters and do a good job for the forest by decomposing the dead wood, returning vital elements and minerals to the ecosystem.

Parasitic mushrooms are as named, living on their host – whether that's a plant, insect or even another mushroom, like the lobster mushroom's takeover of the parasol. The parasitic mushroom embeds itself in a live organism, which it then grows within and takes minerals and nutrients from. Some parasitic mushrooms can cause disease in plants, animals and humans, and we eat only a few.

This complex chart has colour highlights to show which mushrooms share some categories and therefore characteristics. >

	MUSHROOM NAME	DIVISON	CLASS	FAMILY	GENUS	GILLS/ PORES	SEASON
Mycorrhizal	Morel	ascomycota	Pezizomycetes	Morchellaceae	Morchella	pitted	Spring
Mycorrhizal	Black truffle	ascomycota	Pezizomycetes	Tuberaceae	Tuber	none	Summer/Autumn/Winter
Mycorrhizal	White truffle	ascomycota	Pezizomycetes	Tuberaceae	Tuber	none	Autumn/Winter
Mycorrhizal	St George's	basidiomycota	Agaricomycetes	Lyophyllaceae	Calocybe	gills	Spring
Mycorrhizal	Caesar	basidiomycota	Agaricomycetes	Amanitaceae	Amanita	gills	Summer/Autumn
Mycorrhizal	Matsutake	basidiomycota	Agaricomycetes	Tricholomataceae	Tricholoma	gills	Autumn
Mycorrhizal	Pied de mouton	basidiomycota	Agaricomycetes	Hydnaceae	Hydnum	spines	Autumn/Winter
Mycorrhizal	Girolle	basidiomycota	Agaricomycetes	Cantharellaceae	Cantharellus	ridges	Summer
Mycorrhizal	Chanterelle	basidiomycota	Agaricomycetes	Cantharellaceae	Craterellus	ridges	Autumn/Winter
Mycorrhizal	Trompette	basidiomycota	Agaricomycetes	Cantharellaceae	Craterellus	ridges	Autumn/Winter
Mycorrhizal	Cep	basidiomycota	Agaricomycetes	Boletaceae	Boletus	pores	Autumn/Winter
Mycorrhizal	Russula	basidiomycota	Agaricomycetes	Russulaceae	Russula	gills	Autumn
Saprotrophic	Button	basidiomycota	Agaricomycetes	Agaricaceae	Agaricus	gills	Summer/Autumn/ Cultivated
Saprotrophic	Chestnut	basidiomycota	Agaricomycetes	Agaricaceae	Agaricus	gills	Summer/Autumn/ Cultivated
Saprotrophic	Flat	basidiomycota	Agaricomycetes	Agaricaceae	Agaricus	gills	Autumn/Cultivated
Saprotrophic	Portobello	basidiomycota	Agaricomycetes	Agaricaceae	Agaricus	gills	Autumn/Cultivated
Saprotrophic	Horse	basidiomycota	Agaricomycetes	Agaricaceae	Agaricus	gills	Autumn/Cultivated
Saprotrophic	Parasol	basidiomycota	Agaricomycetes	Agaricaceae	Macrolepiota	gills	Autumn
Saprotrophic	Puffball	basidiomycota	Agaricomycetes	Agaricaceae	Various	none	Autumn
Saprotrophic	Shiitake	basidiomycota	Agaricomycetes	Marasmiaceae	Lentinus	gills	Cultivated
Saprotrophic	Enoki	basidiomycota	Agaricomycetes	Physalacriaceae	Flammulina	gills	Autumn/Winter/ Cultivated
Saprotrophic	Nameko	basidiomycota	Agaricomycetes	Strophariaceae	Pholiota	gills	Cultivated
Saprotrophic	Straw	basidiomycota	Agaricomycetes	Pluteaceae	Volvariella	gills	Cultivated
Saprotrophic	Mousseron	basidiomycota	Agaricomycetes	Marasmiaceae	Marasmius	gills	Spring/Autumn
Saprotrophic	Sparassis	basidiomycota	Agaricomycetes	Sparassidaceae	Sparassis	pitted	Autumn/Cultivated
Saprotrophic	Pied bleu	basidiomycota	Agaricomycetes	Tricholomataceae	Lepista	gills	Autumn/Cultivated
Saprotrophic	Shimeji	basidiomycota	Agaricomycetes	Tricholomataceae	Hypsizygus	gills	Cultivated
Saprotrophic	Oyster	basidiomycota	Agaricomycetes	Pleurotaceae	Pleurotus	gills	Autumn/Cultivated
Saprotrophic	Eryngii	basidiomycota	Agaricomycetes	Pleurotaceae	Pleurotus	gills	Autumn/Cultivated
Parasitic	Maitake (or hen of the woods)	basidiomycota	Agaricomycetes	Meripilaceae	Grifola	pores	Autumn/Cultivated
Parasitic	Chicken of the woods	basidiomycota	Agaricomycetes	Fomitopsidaceae	Laetiporus	pores	Autumn
Parasitic	Beef steak mushroom	basidiomycota	Agaricomycetes	Fistulinaceae	Fistulina	pores	Autumn
Parasitic	Lobster	ascomycota	Sordariomycetes	Hypocreaceae	Hypomyces	pores	Autumn

THE CULTIVATION OF MUSHROOMS

Cultivated mushrooms are farmed, rather than being foraged where they grow wild in forests and fields. They are grown in controlled environments like large mushroom factories, so that a constant and higher volume of mushrooms can be produced for our ever-eager palates.

Before mass production of mushrooms began around about the 1900s, mushrooms were still thought of as something unusual and sought-after, with only a few people able to locate and enjoy them. Mushroom cultivation brought mushrooms to the masses.

'Farmed' mushrooms are originally cultivated from spores of wild mushrooms, usually saprotrophic ones, but now spores are reproduced on a massive scale. The process of cultivation has been going on for centuries and in fact some varieties of mushroom, like the cultivated eryngii, has almost become a different mushroom in looks to its wild counterpart. Worldwide and in order of popularity, Agaricus bisporus (closed-cup, button, flat, chestnut and portobello), shiitake mushrooms and oyster mushrooms are the most cultivated, and account for around three-quarters of the global mushroom market.

Fungi cultivation is big business: it's been predicted that the cultivated mushroom market will be worth over 50,000 million dollars by the end of this decade. China is the largest producer, growing 70% of the world's cultivated mushrooms, with the USA and The Netherlands coming in second and third place. The global market for mushrooms was valued at just under 30 million dollars in 2013, so you can see the rapid growth of the industry – much like the growth cycle of the humble mushroom itself.

There are almost two different histories to mushroom cultivation, which separates quite neatly into Eastern or Asian, and Western. Each journey of discovery existed on other sides of the world but rarely worked together or even knew of each other, resulting in a massive array of different mushrooms for us to all enjoy now.

The last century has seen the two mushroom worlds meet and learn from each other. There are now shiitake and oyster mushroom growers in the West, and previously obscure Asian mushrooms like eryngii and shimeji are becoming popular in both supermarkets and restaurants; similarly Western mushrooms have been incorporated into the fusion food emerging in the East, especially when it comes to truffles. The demand for mushrooms and mushroom products will continue to rise. Mycology, the study of mushrooms, is ongoing, and who knows where the wonderful world of mushroom cultivation will take us next. There are sure to be many tasty ideas on the horizon, too...

Cultivated mushrooms, clockwise from top left: oyster, portobello, button, enoki, golden enoki, chestnut, maitake, shimeji, eryngii, pied bleu, shimeji and shiitake. >

EASTERN MUSHROOM GROWING

Asia has a long and rich tradition of mushroom cultivation and the mushrooms are beautiful and refined, as well as nutritionally and medically beneficial. In Japan, China and Korea, mushrooms such as eryngii, shiitake, shimeji, enoki and nameko are grown on a massive scale. These Asian or 'exotic' types of mushrooms are becoming more popular in the West, as supermarkets increasingly sell a range of mixed punnets, but these mushrooms can seem far removed from the mushrooms Europeans grew up eating.

The first written record of growing Japanese mushrooms dates back to 1209, with details of labourers encouraging shiitake mushrooms to grow on wooden logs – a process now called 'selective logging'. Shii tree logs were cut and placed alongside shiitakes growing naturally on decaying wood on hillsides, and the spores would then transplant themselves, doubling or tripling the crop.

This simple and natural method developed, with stacked inoculated logs used to grow mushrooms like nameko, oyster, pom pom, wood ears and reishi. Trees such as alder, poplar or cottonwood were inoculated and stacked for six months, then soaked with water and lined up near shiitake logs, so the spores spread in an airborne way. This is known as the 'soak and strike' method, as the next step is to hit the logs to 'shock' the mycelium or spores into producing fruit.

A lot of mushrooms were and are still grown by selective logging, however in the 20th century new techniques and technologies led to the development of purpose-built facilities producing mushrooms on blocks or jars of sterilized substrate. Mushrooms are now grown on unnatural sterilized habitat or substrate such as cereal straws, corncobs, seed hulls, sugarcane bagasse, paper, pulp and even coffee waste, but usually agricultural and forestry by-products. Factories have conveyor belts of glass jars, filled with the substrate and mycelium from which mushroom caps pop out from the top. It is a sea of hundreds of thousands of jars, carefully moved within different temperature- and humidity-controlled environments for the growing stages.

The big benefit for any chef or home cook of Asian cultivated mushrooms is that they are consistent and mostly clean. These are mushrooms with looks and texture – and that visual 'wow' factor.

Eastern mushrooms, clockwise from top left: golden enoki, brown and white shimeji, shiitake, white enoki, eryngii and oyster. >

WESTERN MUSHROOM GROWING

Western cultivation methods are slightly different, with the growing matter of choice being compost – probably because of the way field mushrooms grow – embodied with mycelium. Agaricus bisporus, now the most common mushroom type, with button, closed-cup, flat, chestnut and portobello, was the first species to be cultivated in this way.

As with the shii logs on the other side of the world, cultivation didn't start in labs or growing facilities. It is said that in the 17th century a French melon grower first accidentally discovered that he had grown edible mushrooms on melon fertilizer. The story has it that this melon farmer started to sell his accidental mushrooms to chefs in Paris, coining the phrase the Paris or Parisian Mushroom, which despite its grand name is simply the button mushroom we have today, pulled out of the ground rather than cut at the stalk, and sold with a muddy bottom.

It was around this time that mushroom cultivation began in caves in France, mostly in and around Paris, as growers realized that the cool, damp and relatively controlled environment suited larger scale mushroom production. From here until the start of the 1900s, cave cultivation was the main mode of mushroom growing in the West, until things got technical.

In the meantime, the USA had began mushroom cultivation around the mid 1800s, importing mycelium from England, and the Dutch had also begun what would be their ongoing love affair with mushroom production, taking the simple closed-cup mushroom from rare exclusivity to an accessible commodity available in every supermarket. By 1934 we had the first scientific study of mushroom culture from the Research Station, Naaldwijk in The Netherlands, and in 1950 their first above-ground growing facility was created, which eventually led to the multi-tier units. Housed in large farming rooms in 30 metre-long aluminum shelves, the various Agaricus bisporus types now grow separately in sterilized compost with controlled temperature, cooling and water vapour, to produce a mushroom crop ready for market in a couple of weeks.

< Western mushrooms, clockwise from top: flat, closed-cup, pied bleu, chestnut, yellow oyster, oyster and, in the centre, button and shiitake.

FORAGING FOR MUSHROOMS

There is a very romantic notion of mushroom foraging. For years, mostly in mainland Europe where there are comparatively easy pickings, it has been a normal activity or pastime. A lot of us have memories of mushroom foraging when we were young, but just a few, or a basketful.

Local foraging knowledge is passed down, and whole families often spend a weekend mushroom foraging together, getting fresh air and exercise in the meantime, then cooking up a meal and preserving the extra for the weeks ahead. There are forests and areas that are known for good pickings, although this is all now changing to a certain extent with restrictions coming into place due to commercial overpicking.

However, to have mushrooms in volume to supply a large catering or retail market, it's a full-time job come autumn and winter and the reality is that commercial foragers are well organised. The wild mushrooms we eat in our restaurants and buy are mostly due to a network of rather silent and hidden well-timed operations throughout the world.

A good professional chef understands that mushroom availability can be changeable, with weather dictating sometimes very short mushroom seasons and with wild patches ending their growing flushes abruptly; sometimes a mushroom can be available one day, then not being seen again for another year. Nonetheless the mushroom selling game can get very fast and frantic, especially in late summer and early autumn when chefs and food markets want the next just-available wild mushroom.

Cue the mushroom forager. Sometimes reclusive and preferring to keep themselves to themselves, a lot of mushroom foragers are very secretive about their coveted patches and areas, and the best are respectful of the environment and pick carefully so as not to rip up root systems, and make it easier for the new spores to spread. After all, the sustainability and continuation of various wild mushrooms is their livelihood. From autumn to winter, forests are a way of life for a commercial forager but one thing's for sure, you've got to really love mushrooms. At the right time of year and for the best mushrooms, foraging can be very lucrative and unfortunately this can bring out less scrupulous short-term pickers. Michael is as careful in choosing his foragers to supply wild mushrooms as he is in the commercial suppliers of cultivated mushrooms.

THE GUIDE TO MUSHROOMS

HOW TO USE THIS DIRECTORY

There are many different varieties and types of edible mushrooms out there – more than 2,300 it's thought – and with this overwhelming choice, it's hard to know where to start when it comes to choosing the mushroom you'd like to cook for supper.

Our mushroom directory helps with a longlist of the best edible mushrooms that are generally available or likely to be spotted at a market. We excluded lesser-used edible varieties and focussed on those that you are likely to find, whether in supermarket punnets, in delicatessens and greengrocers, and in farmer's markets. Some mushrooms profiled are popular and commonly found, a few are rarer ones you might be more lucky to come across, so grab them when you do.

Ordered by seasonal availability, the directory details all of the mushrooms we have used in our recipes and a few that we haven't, but all of them are what we consider the more interesting for the kitchen. There are around 40 types catalogued, from your everyday closed-cup mushroom to the more elusive and expensive. Whether you have bought a punnet of chanterelles at your local market that you want to find out more about before you cook, or you're interested in reading about the startling parasitic and fish-like lobster mushroom in the hope of purchasing it one day, the directory tells you all about the individual mushrooms: where they are grown; the other (sometimes many) names they hail by throughout the world; what they look like and how their appearance might change as they age through the seasons; their variations of taste and texture; storage advice; how to clean and prepare them; and suggestions for dishes and ingredient pairings they are perfect for, with cross-references to recipes to try them in.

We have separated our mushroom profiles into those that are mainly picked wild and those that are grown commercially. Of course, this isn't an exact science – all mushrooms that are grown in facilities have come from a wild version of themselves in the first place. For example, oyster mushrooms can be found growing from tree barks in forests almost anywhere in their season, but they are so easy to grow in an controlled environment that when we buy oyster mushrooms this is more than likely where they come from. For that reason they feature in our cultivated section, as do most of the Agaricus family, with the exception of their mainly wild counterparts like the field mushroom, from which our everyday favourite the flat mushroom derives.

Safety in mushroom identification and eating is paramount, and our book focuses on the mushrooms you can buy, rather than as a guide for foragers in the wild.

PARTS OF A MUSHROOM

No two mushroom types are quite the same, but their division, class, family and genus (see pages 10-11) can mean they have similar characteristics, such as gills, ridges, pores and/or spines. Some mushrooms have typical features; some do not. Some features can be present but more or less obviously, and their appearance can change of course with age.

Some (and note, many poisonous) mushrooms grow from a volva, produced by the mushroom's mycelium; from the volva, the universal veil grows, protecting the mushroom's fruiting body growing inside, which finally bursts out of the veil into a stem and cap, usually featuring gills underneath, from which the spores are dispersed. Mushrooms either have gills, ridges, spines (also known as tubes), pits, pores or none of those at all!

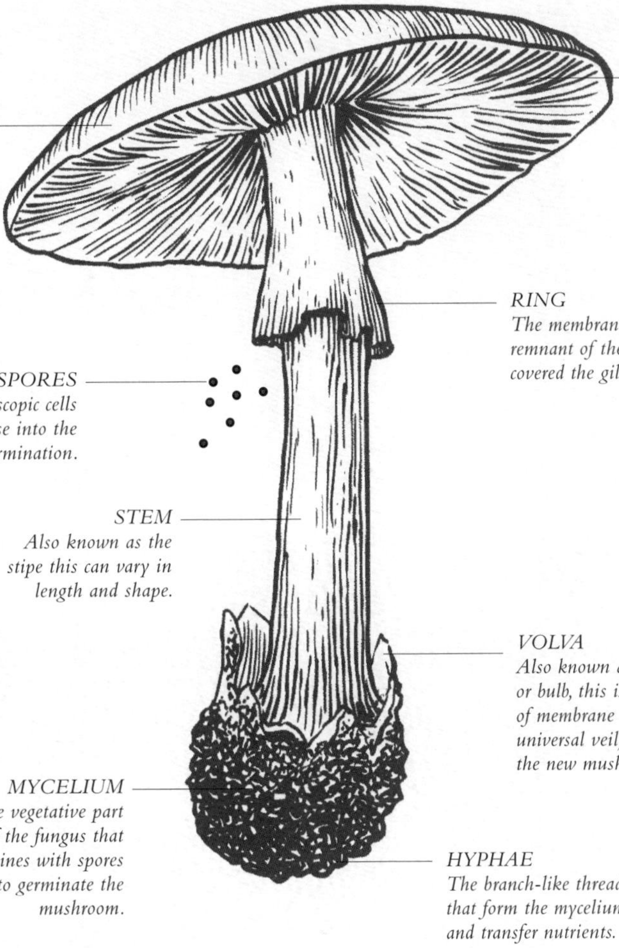

WILD MUSHROOMS

Morel THE SUPERMODEL

OTHER NAMES
Dryland fish, molly moochers, hickory hens, merkels, sponge mushroom

LATIN NAMES
Morchella vulgaris, Morchella esculenta, Morchella elata

USUALLY FOUND IN
UK, Europe, the USA, Canada, Tibet

SEASON
March to July

The mighty morel shows up loud and proud amongst forest floors around about March and heralds spring in abundance all over the northern hemisphere. The morel has many variations, differing only slightly from each other, with the black morel, yellow morel and white morel being the most commonly known and coveted throughout Europe and the USA. As soon as January hits, we are thinking about these little black to off-white, almost tree-like, mushrooms and hoping for an early start.

This mushroom looks like no other: its brilliant-white hollow stem is where any similarities with other fungi end, as what grows on top of it is a black to sometimes grey to white oval dome of intricate crevices, looking a little like a sea coral or honeycomb, with the texture of a young or pickled walnut. They look fantastical, as if an alien life-force or little distorted candle flames have taken over the forest – and they are key in the wild mushroom calendar as the first prized and precious mushroom of any real commercial availability in the year.

The first flush is from China, then the first European flush usually starts in Turkey, which has a long season, but you can then find morels throughout Europe until early summer, until the USA and Canada see the season out to July, depending as ever on the weather. Demand for morels has always been high across Europe and the USA, and has increased dramatically in the UK over the last 15 years, as people become more accustomed to a larger array of wild mushrooms.

Tricky to find, morels are usually camouflaged by their natural environment. They grow amongst dead leaves left over from winter or in little nooks and crannies at the base of forest trees, where they find the best moisture and shade from the springtime sun. A thing of beauty, popping up either singularly or in spaced-out mini clusters of two or threes amongst decomposing winter leaves, foragers have to get close up to the ground to even see them most of the time. It's backbreaking work that has to be done in the precious few daylight hours of early spring. But like the supermodel mushroom it is, the morel is worth it and they shine out like little beacons to those in the know.

One of the mycorrhizal mushrooms, morels have a very strong relationship with trees and grow in unison with the roots, sharing nutrients. As with many mushrooms, morels have been known to pop up in the same place for years. It has been recently discovered that morels also fruit just after forest fires on burn sites, leading to some commercial foragers in the USA and Finland, in particular, taking to the 'slash and burn' approach to encourage morel growth. Despite the questionable success of this and its implications on the natural environment, commercial morel cultivation has been proved near-impossible so far, although the mushrooms are great acclimatisers themselves, appearing in urban settings like gardens and green areas where rotting wood resides.

> *continues overleaf*

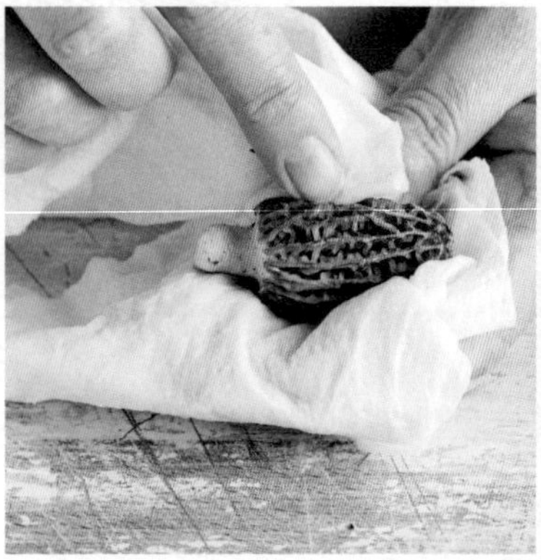

Storage:
When morels are a little past their best they either start to dry out or collapse, becoming moist and deteriorating quickly. If you get freshly picked morels, they can last a week, but as with all mushrooms, and especially wild ones, it is best to eat them as soon as you can.

Nutrition:
Morels contain vitamin B and D, potassium and niacin.

PREPARATION AND COOKING

The morel is completely different to any of the main wild mushrooms we eat, which is probably why it is so fascinating, both in the forest and on the plate. Intricate but sturdy, it's a mushroom 'in-betweener' that needs a certain amount of cooking to make it edible (it's poisonous raw) and has a distinct, strong and nutty flavour.

As you can probably tell, morels are a bit high-maintenance to clean and it has to be a labour of love if you are preparing to eat quite a few of them. The wonderfully pretty, brain-like cap is also a popular home for a whole host of creepy crawlies and dirt. To prepare a morel, it's a good idea to hold it over some kitchen paper and give it a couple of gentle taps so that the majority of unwelcome visitors and dirt are removed straightaway. Using a small paintbrush or tweezers, pick out the remaining bits and bobs you don't want out of the morel's pocketed flesh. Take a cold damp cloth or piece of kitchen roll and wipe the whole mushroom.

Cut the morel in half lengthways and wipe the insides gently. Alternatively, in some of our recipes we slice vertically (see the morel and shimeji flatbreads on page 136 and Portuguese wild mushroom risotto on page 130), which makes for a pretty flower shape. Some chefs breadcrumb and fry the mushrooms whole, which negates the chopping open and cleaning them, but we recommend always cleaning and slicing.

Chefs love these little mushroom morsels that offer a delicate taste of the woods and a unique texture, and they find their way into sauces, stews, pies, casseroles and pasta dishes. Making a good pairing with creamy sauces and dishes, morels are also tasty with game and rich meats. We have teamed them up with duck livers for a smooth and rich-flavoured pâté recipe on page 132, included them in meaty wild boar sausages (page 138), a spring focaccia (page 128) and a pulled rabbit ravioli (page 124).

St George's mushroom THE OPPORTUNIST

OTHER NAMES
Maipilz, marzolino

LATIN NAME
Calocybe gambosa

USUALLY FOUND IN
UK, Italy France, Spain, Bulgaria and throughout Europe, Russia, Asia, the USA

SEASON
April to May/June

Storage:
Store St George's in the refrigerator, in an open plastic container or a loosely fastened paper bag. Keep them dry and use within a week.

Nutrition:
A source of vitamin D, St George's are thought to have anti-bacterial qualities through the dichloromethane compound said to be active against some bacteria, and to also reduce blood sugar levels.

The St George's mushroom is a perfectly formed archetypal mushroom. White and firm, with a small stem and cute petite cap, it is popular because, like the morel, its arrival signifies a certain time of year, and is greatly anticipated even though its season is short. First off the block in spring, certainly in England and Ireland, and an early mushroom for the rest of Europe, St George's pops up in all its splendour around St George's Day on 23rd April – hence its very British name. This mushroom isn't exclusive to the British Isles though; its name stays the same around Europe, with the understanding that this fungi was a 'gift' from that generous fellow, the patron saint of England, Saint George. However, there are some places that use their own names according to the months the mushroom appears in the wild in that country – in Italy it's marzolino (March mushroom) and in Germany it's called maipilz (May mushroom).

A firm, strong and proud-looking gilled mushroom, the first St George's are picked very young, when their caps are so tight that there are hardly any gills to be seen. Picked medium-sized, the mushroom is shown off to its best advantage and opens up to a perfectly formed upside-down cap shape. Creamy white in colour and with a slight chalky taste, St George's is vaguely similar to pied bleu visually, but whiter and with a more intense forest-like flavour.

St George's mushrooms would perhaps struggle to be as popular in the autumn, when much better-tasting and smarter-looking mushrooms are around, but this asparagus of the mushroom world is a sought-after little number that creates quite a buzz among chefs. Foragers are so keen to collect it that the first pickings or flush of the mushroom can seem like a different type of mushroom compared to its fuller grown form later in the month. This first flush is picked very young, and the first to arrive are often pinhead-small. It is a bit sad if nothing has arrived by the 23rd, but the season will start when the weather dictates. Whenever it does begin and whatever volumes there are (quantities can be very low depending on the weather conditions), the demand is there from day one because chefs want to start their spring menus. Where the mushroom grows wild in abundance, like Italy, France and Spain, it is eaten up by the home market. However, Bulgaria has seen a keen export market for its foraged St George's in recent years.

Caution:
Collecting immature mushrooms must be done by very experienced foragers. Beginners can very easily confuse an immature poisonous species for an edible one.

PREPARATION AND COOKING

Especially if they have not been spattered by the rain, St George's mushrooms are a joy to clean compared to some smaller, more delicate characters, as their dry, sturdy nature and lack of intricate crevices mean they are less likely to fall apart, and there's no delving for hidden bits and pieces of dirt and leaves. In fact, especially with the younger specimens, their gills are so close together that hardly anything can get in there. To clean, hold the mushroom by its cap and gently brush any dirt away from its gills. Take a cold damp cloth or kitchen paper and wipe away any dirt from the cap and stem. Trim the stem, then slice as needed. Some of the recipes in this book call for whole St George's mushrooms, so do check the instructions first.

Because of its season and first billing on the mushroom menu, St George is commonly used in traditional dishes, such as pâté, on toast and in tarts, and paired with other seasonal offerings like wild garlic, asparagus, purple sprouting broccoli and their spring mushroom rival morels. Due to their dry nature, St George's take a little longer to cook than your common closed-cup mushroom and benefit from a little extra cooking oil or stock.

Although their smell can be quite distinct, when they are cooked they have a light and delicate fungi taste. Our mushrooms in oil recipe (page 142) really makes the most of both the mushroom's taste and firm texture, keeping them whole and preserving them with salt and in a lightly flavoured oil. They also feature in the Portuguese wild mushroom risotto (page 130) and are an intrinsic part of the spring wild mushroom sausages (page 138).

Mousseron A TEAM PLAYER

OTHER NAMES
Fairy ring, Scotch bonnet

LATIN NAME
Marasmius oreades

USUALLY FOUND IN
UK, Europe, the USA, Canada

SEASON
April to May, then September to October

Storage:
Store in an open plastic container in the refrigerator for no longer than a week.

Nutrition:
Mousserons contain amino acids, copper, iron, zinc, folic acid and protein.

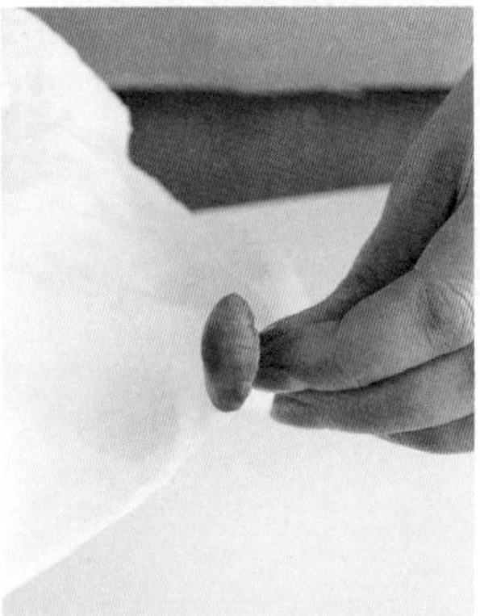

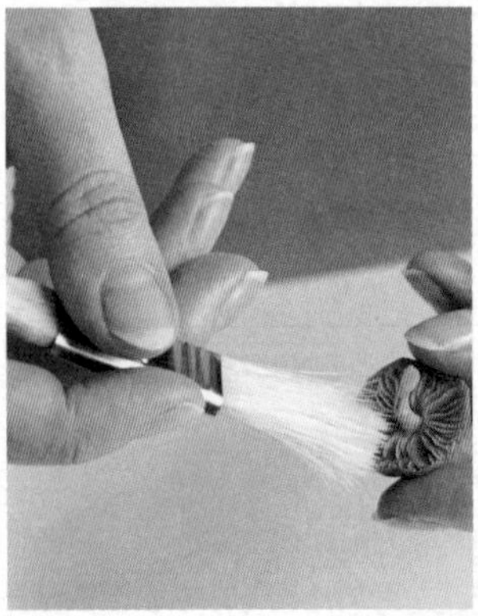

Surrounded by mystery for centuries, mousserons are the perfect natural props for any fairytale. Rumoured to be prevalent throughout the Stonehenge circle, mousserons belong to the family Marasmius, which are all known as 'fairy ring mushrooms' because they often grow together in circles. Many folk laws and legends imbue these light-brown mushrooms with significance, with some suggesting they are the work of fairies themselves, when of course in fact they are connected by a ecological system below the grass they grow on. The French name 'mousseron' simply means to grow on moss.

The size of daisies and very similar to small flowers in a number of ways, mousserons are maybe only 5cm/2in high and have either flat or slightly umbrella-like caps that are not much bigger in width. They are very delicate, so much so that the cap really is just a thin film covering the top of the gills. Foragers have to be careful in many respects when picking mousserons, due to their fragile nature and closeness to the ground, but importantly because they are part of a huge family thought to have no fewer than 500 species, with more than 30 species in the UK, but of which only a few are known to be edible. On the positive side, edible mousserons are quite distinctive in comparison with others in their family and grow in abundance at the end of spring or start of summer and through to mid-autumn.

Mousserons grow all over Europe, starting off in spring just after St George's in the Balkan countries, if the weather is typical. It's relatively easy to find a lot, because of the often large rings they grow in. There is also a small commercial availability of mousseron's cousin, the amethyst deceiver, which is also known as the purple mousseron. Its cap shape is more a uniformed umbrella than the mousseron and it has a striking flavour to match its colour. Mousserons have a very strong smell – like a very intense forest scent or wooden aroma – and their nectar-ish taste is reminiscent of this, although not as strong, making them great for stocks and soups. But it's visually where mousseron finds its place in the culinary world. These cute little grassland morsels can make a plate as pretty as a picture.

PREPARATION AND COOKING
As attractive as they are, mousserons are one of those troublesome mushrooms that makes you work for your dinner, and it might be easier for the cook to get some help if you're planning on cooking a lot of these. First, take a piece of kitchen paper and place it on a chopping board, then give the mushroom a gentle tap, so most of the dirt falls out. Gently wipe the tops with a damp cloth, then use a small paintbrush or a pair of tweezers to remove any stubborn pieces of dirt.

Use the mushrooms whole in recipes, or roughly chop, if you wish. They make up for all the cleaning by being delicate and small, and therefore taking no time at all to cook. Mousserons are often paired with chicken in casseroles and sauces, and their richer than usual umami taste makes them a great addition to game or vegetarian dishes. We have put them in a tart (page 134), preserved them in oil (page 142), and pan-fried them with butter and honey as part of a salad (page 156).

Girolle THE JACKPOT

OTHER NAMES
Chanterelle, golden chanterelle

LATIN NAME
Cantharellus cibarius

USUALLY FOUND IN
Scotland and England, Eastern Europe, Spain, Portugal

SEASON
All year, but best in summer

Like little pots of gold on the forest floor, girolles burst onto the scene after a mushroom drought in the wild.

As spring goes into summer, the first flush of girolles are suddenly in abundance. Tiny golden shoots spring up, growing in a trail of little clusters that follow on for what seems like forever, making them pleasant to forage and resulting in nice full baskets for chefs, greengrocers and markets, who all keenly await them.

Especially pretty on the plate and flower-like in form, the mushrooms are trumpet-like in stature and range from pale yellow to light orange, with a smooth or inverted top and small delicate, vein-like ridges trailing up in higgledy-piggledy manner to the sky from a thick stem. Firm but with a softness, the mushroom grows amongst moss and decomposing leaves, amongst beech, oak or pine trees. Foragers are wary of a 'false chanterelle' which is very similar, although a little flatter on the cap and darker in colour, as it can cause stomach upsets as well as having less flavour.

Girolles share similarities with the yellow and grey trumpet chanterelles and trompette, and are sometimes called golden chanterelles as a result. Until recently these four mushrooms had all been classed as one happy family, but molecular phylogenetics has now established that the yellow and grey chanterelles and trompette are quite different from the girolles.

As a result of its long season, the girolle has an ever-changing face, and its appearance differs slightly throughout the season, according to the weather and where it grows. The summer and winter girolles can look quite different to one another, but the archetypal girolle is that of the new-season mushroom of the summer. Supply of this starts with girolles from Eastern Europe (usually Serbia), continues to a Scottish season popular with British chefs mid-summer to early autumn, then to Portuguese and Spanish girolles in early to late winter and early spring, and with US supply coming in to the end. The new-season always looks beautiful and is very much in demand.

As it's quite pleasing on the eye to have three or four petite orange girolles on your plate, chefs are keen on the first flushes of girolles. Known as mini girolles, these first flushes are still virtually pinheads, and are young and tender. On the other side of the fence, the older flourishing girolles have a more developed flavour, so this culinary decision seems mainly aesthetic. Girolles grow rather rapidly, so mini girolles are harder to find in time and cost more to pick, as their weight will be much less.

> *continues overleaf*

Storage:
Girolles are a strong mushroom that will keep in the refrigerator just past a week from picking, but are best as fresh as possible.

Nutrition:
Girolles are a good source of vitamin D, and also contain iron and copper.

PREPARATION AND COOKING

In comparison with some more delicate and spindly mushrooms, girolles are quite easy to clean. Take a clean, damp cloth and gently wipe the tops, then brush or wipe any dirt away from the ridges. Rather than clean, chefs tend to peel them from the top of the stem down with the back of a knife, to create a long clean stem. Mini girolles are usually cooked whole and you can rip a full-sized one into quarters or chop finely.

Some say girolles are reminiscent of apricots, but whatever you can taste, they are fresh and light, with chefs opting to use them for sauces and delicate garnishes. Usually pan-fried, they are also good grilled with only a light coating of oil and can be caramelised on their own. They will need a little extra cooking because of their robustness. Great with red meat and fish, we have used them as a tasty addition to our gourmet mushroom burger (page 170), pan-fried them in whisky and baked with black pudding for our Belfast breakfast (page 166 and not for the faint-hearted), and served them with our fillet steak (page 210).

Dryad's saddle THE OFF-CHANCE

OTHER NAMES
Pheasant's back, hawk's wing, scaly polypore

LATIN NAMES
Polyporus squamosus, Cerioporus squamosus

USUALLY FOUND IN
Europe, Asia, Australia, the USA

SEASON
May to June

Storage:
It is recommended that you eat this mushroom straight away as it loses its aroma and taste within a day of picking.

Nutrition:
The dryad's saddle is said to speed up the metabolism.

Almost as mystical as its fairytale namesake, the dryad's saddle is common in the wild, but it has virtually no commercial availability. If you do happen to get your hands on it at a market, farmers' market or deli, which will no doubt be the result of a forager's random find whilst looking for something else with more demand, it's fascinating to both cook and eat.

You may have seen them in children's books; not as food, but literally as seats for pixies or dryads (otherwise known as tree nymph in folklore), hence the name. Visually a little bird-like, this fan-shaped mushroom has large brown scales rather like feathers on top of it, and grows out the bark of trees, much like the oyster mushroom.

Growing across Europe, Asia and the USA, the fungi makes its home mainly on hardwood trees. Younger versions of this huge (sometimes up to 30cm/12in wide) mushroom are preferred for eating, as older examples can be tough and are probably already being devoured by slugs. The eating season is May to June, but they do grow to around August, although they are not considered especially edible past June. Reminiscent of chicken of the woods, it is said by some to smell of watermelon rind (although that's not something we pick up on) and has a soft texture, a lot like a puffball.

PREPARATION AND COOKING

The dryad's saddle is very easy to prepare. Just wipe clean with some damp kitchen paper, cut off any very hard stem or scales, and slice. You can cover the slices lightly with tempura batter using our recipe on page 186 or make the most of their brilliant-white flesh in a grilled summer salad (page 156). Some people enjoy pickling them, others make a teriyaki dish out of them or serve with osso buco. Whatever you do, make sure you cook this mushroom thoroughly as undercooking can use stomach upsets for some people.

Chanterelle PRETTY THINGS

OTHER NAMES
Yellow foot, grey foot, winter chanterelle, flame-coloured chanterelle, small chanterelle, trumpet or funnel chanterelle

LATIN NAMES
Craterellus tubaeformis, Craterellus lutescens

USUALLY FOUND IN
UK, Europe, the USA, Scandinavia, Russia

SEASON
July to March

Visually spectacular, firm and versatile and slightly sweet in taste, grey and yellow chanterelles are always popular in restaurants and people love the look of them. The grey and yellow chanterelles are two different species of the same family with separate Latin names, but are generally known as yellow foot and grey foot or winter chanterelles. Tasting pretty much the same, they are only very slightly different in looks – both have small umbrella-like yellow-grey caps and long thin hollow stems (referred to as legs or foots), so the only real difference is the colour of their stems, which are either grey or yellow. The grey chanterelle can be a little sturdier, whereas the yellow is usually a bit smaller, more delicate and more prone to moisture, but in general they are both light and spindly mushrooms that grow up to 7.5cm/3in tall in groups on the forest floor in the late summer and throughout the autumn into winter.

Historically, the chanterelles have always been linked to the girolle, with which they share the characteristics of small and intricate wrinkled and veiny ridges instead of gills, but taxonomists have recently pushed them out of the girolle family tree and classified them as a Craterellus – the same family group as the trompette mushroom (see page 58). Growing on moss or rotting woods, the yellow and grey chanterelle's trumpet-shaped beacons first appear in France in midsummer and can be found from as early as July throughout Europe, Canada and the USA, through to March in the USA. These flower-like mushrooms have a high-water content and thrive in muggy damp conditions, but they don't cope well when the temperature drops in the winter. They disappear with the first frost, but are readily available for almost half of the year, or longer if conditions say mild. Like a lot of wild mushrooms, chanterelles are good at camouflage, but grow in great numbers together, so once found, commercial foragers usually have a decent volume to sell.

The pretty face of the mushroom world, chanterelles are aesthetically pleasing in dishes and are one of the most-used mainstream wild mushrooms in professional kitchens throughout Europe. More chefs ask for yellow, even though grey has a better shelf life, but in general it's about provenance – French, Scottish or Scandinavian chanterelles have the most prestige with chefs much like the Italian cep or Perigord truffle.

> *continues overleaf*

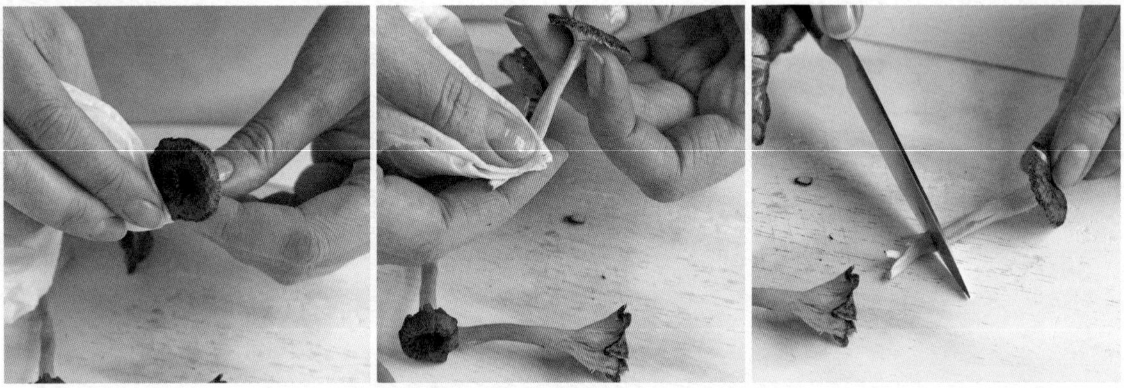

Storage:
The grey lasts slightly longer than the yellow, but in general, they will keep in the refrigerator, in open plastic containers, for a week. As they are prone to wet, it is best not to cover them with plastic or store near something that could leak. These mushrooms dry well and are popular in that form in Scandinavian countries.

Nutrition:
It is said that both grey and yellow chanterelles are particularly rich in vitamin D.

PREPARATION AND COOKING

Some extra care needs to be taken when it comes to cleaning chanterelles and they must never be washed in water. Instead, take a damp cloth or piece of kitchen roll and wipe the tops gently to remove any dirt. Then wrap the cloth around the stem and move it down to the end to clean completely. Remove the end as it can be come tough in transit. You can cook the mushroom whole, or ripped in half lengthways from the tip of the stalk to the end.

Chanterelles have the slightly sweet taste of autumnal forests and are often sautéed and added to a dish more as a garnish than an ingredient to bulk out a meal, like the pied de mouton or field mushroom. Soft and delicate, they don't need a lot of cooking and are popular in sauces, soups (like our chanterelle, truffle and chestnut soup on page 188) and stews. They go particularly well with creamy sauces and game birds, like partridge (see the stew on page 224) and pheasant.

On top of their aesthetic qualities, chanterelles also have a soft, delicate texture. A different creature to the sturdy cep or girolle, the chanterelle is pleasingly stringy with an almost petal-like soft cap, more like the cultivated enoki mushroom (see page 92). They are best, like most mushrooms, simply grilled with a little oil and served on bread with various accompaniments (see our mushroom tapas recipe on page 214), or roughly churned in a quick mushroom and sherry pâté (page 218). We have also used them in a chunky wild mushroom and brandy butter sauce for a fillet steak (page 210), and a fresh-tasting sea bass baked in vine leaves (on page 194).

Caesar THE FILMSTAR

OTHER NAMES
Ovolo, ovolo buono, fungo reale, oronge

LATIN NAME
Amanita caesarea

USUALLY FOUND IN
Southern Europe, Bulgaria, Africa

SEASON
June to late summer

Fetching a high price in Italy, Spain and France and thought to be the early rulers of the Roman Empire's favourite mushrooms, the caesar mushroom certainly lives up to all the hype and is one of those culinary treats that everyone should try at least once.

Native to southern Europe and North Africa, the mushrooms picked early in the season or developmental growth are a beautifully formed deep-orange egg shape, unlike any other mushroom. Perhaps adding to their mystique, you'd be forgiven for thinking it wasn't a mushroom, that is until you slice it open and find perfectly preserved and protected light orange or yellow gills and a yellow stem. One of the most visually spectacular wild mushrooms around, the caesar is generally picked at two stages of its fruiting or growing cycle – giving it two different looks.

Outfit number one – the chef's preferred caesar – is what the Italians call the 'oval', which roughly translates to the egg shape, where the cap is just about to bulge out of its veil and come to maturity. A known delicacy in Tuscany, the young mushroom is enveloped by a 'universal veil', which is basically membranous tissue, rather like the consistency of a puffball that temporarily covers the mushroom as it grows. It's a good stage to get, because – apart from having distinctly more delicate, fluffy and light gills, and being great for eating raw – it's guaranteed to be clean inside. Quite a rare claim in the mushroom world and worth paying money for...

The mature version of the caesar and the second outfit, is just as good flavour-wise, but looks quite different, as we all do with age. It opens up to a full-capped mushroom, with a far-reaching top, revealing a ring (a circle of membrane-tissue attached to the stem and originally part of the veil) and bright yellow, deep and thin gills that are attached to the thin film top only and have a slightly jagged edge. It looks more like an average capped-mushroom shape and is usually cut from the ground with the mound of leftover protective veil at the bottom, known as the volva. The caesar varies in size at both maturity stages; it might be not much bigger than your average closed-cup mushroom or grow to near the size of a flat mushroom.

Because it is prized in its egg-like form, the perfect caesar is hard to find. It's almost random where it decides to pop up and, as with all basidiomycete agaric types (see page 11) of mushroom, the caesar will grow wherever its spores land and survive. It isn't common in northern Europe, although it has been found in the Balkan peninsula, and it has been found in China, India and Mexico. Nevertheless, it's in the ground of Italian woods and the forests of northern Spain, Hungary, Romania and Bulgaria amongst pine and oak trees that it thrives, with markets in Bologna, Sicily, San Sebastian and Barcelona going crazy for their homegrown delicacy. Compared to the well-known ceps or summer girolles, this little egg-shaped mushroom is a rare find on both UK and USA markets. Depending on where they come from and the weather that year, caesar generally appear in July at a very small size and sometimes last through to October, but are sporadic in availability and form.

> *continues overleaf*

Storage:
These mushrooms keep for up to a week chilled in a plastic container, but more importantly, the best experience is to eat them as fresh as possible, especially if you are eating them raw.

Nutrition:
Caesar mushrooms contain antioxidants, fatty acids and are said to help build the immune system.

PREPARATION AND COOKING

Caesar mushrooms are a real joy to both prepare and eat. As mentioned, the younger egg-shaped mushroom takes hardly any cleaning, and once the outside of the mushroom has been cleaned, you can pretty much slice or chop without investigating with a brush or tweezers.

To clean inside the enclosed caesar, take a damp clean cloth or kitchen paper and gently rub the dirt from the veil (the white stuff growing from the bottom). If it is very dirty, or if you prefer, you can gently peel the first thin layer of the veil, revealing white fluffy veil underneath. Next take a wet cloth to the top orange dome, and clean in a circular motion. It will become sticky as it is cleaned, so be careful you don't put it next to a dirty mushroom as the dirt will stick to it again.

From here you can slice lengthways for a fabulous circular pattern and eat raw in a salad or roast whole. The bright yellow large gills can be pulled apart easily to make a flaky pile, which look a bit like grated butter or flower petals, and can make a plate look weird and wonderful all at the same time.

Preparing the more mature version of the mushroom is very similar, although obviously it has quite a different form. Clean in the same way, making sure the orange top, which will still be sticky, is thoroughly wiped. You will have to do a quick check of the gills for dirt and bugs. You can do this will a small paintbrush by stroking the bits outwards or with tweezers. Before you start, hold the mushroom upright and give the cup a very gentle tap to let the dirt naturally fall.

Taste-wise, they are as pleasing on the palate as they are on the eye, especially when they are raw, when their delicate sweet, nutty and sometimes chestnut-like flavour is intense and the texture is almost velvety. Our caesar mushroom and globe artichoke boats (see page 196) makes the most of these young fungi morsels in an exciting foodie adventure.

Cep THE KING OF THE FOREST

OTHER NAMES
Porcini, penny bun, boletus, king bolete

LATIN NAME
Boletus edulis

USUALLY FOUND IN
UK, Italy, France, Poland, Romania, Portugal, Ukraine, Spain, South Africa, the USA, Mexico

SEASON
June to March

Ceps are the pretty-much undisputed king of the fungi family. Fetching a high price at the height of their season, which runs from June through to March but peaking in the autumn time, ceps are the must-have autumnal mushroom for chefs around the Western world. With a large moist, rich-chestnut colour cap and a strong, thick creamy stem, the cep has yellow pores instead of gills, which change through age to sometimes appear grey or green, and is picked young, before the forager's main competitor, the maggot, gets there first.

It's arguably the visual quality of ceps that makes them so special to both the mushroom and culinary world. With an iconic and unmistakable appearance, it's the archetypical mushroom. Apparently a favourite with the ancient Romans, the cep is the best, wild and natural form of a mushroom – you can't cultivate it, so you have to completely rely on nature.

Ceps are commercially foraged in their tons in European countries from June, but the best quality is September and October, when the weather is colder and fruiting is stronger. In the summer, they are more at the mercy of aforementioned enemy the maggots, which make a cosy home for themselves by laying their eggs in the fungus and then making their way up through the cep as it grows, making it an even harder job for foragers to get a good consistency of quality. You mostly don't know if the maggots have got to the mushroom at the picking stage, so this is why you may find sliced or halved ceps for sale in the summer, to indicate that they are maggot-less. If you ever want to make sure a cep is maggot free, get them from South Africa, but on the downside it's been said these ceps don't have the same flavour.

Known to the Italians as porcini and to some as penny bun, ceps grow in mixed woodland, tree plantations and pathways, growing alongside and intertwining with tree roots throughout the northern hemisphere. It seems people have always recognised the wonders of the cep in Italy, Spain and France, but the UK and the USA have been a little slow to the mushroom party, with demand only really picking up into big business over the last 20 years.

When you buy dried mushrooms in the shops, the likelihood is that it is ceps you are buying, usually labelled as porcini.

> *continues overleaf*

Storage:
Ceps are quite sturdy and are less likely to become squidgy than a more delicate mushroom, but because dormant maggots may still be present in their stalks, it is best to eat them as fresh as possible. However, stored in a plastic tub, spaced a little apart from each other so they do not make each other soggy, they can last in the refrigerator up until a week.

Nutrition:
Ceps are high in protein, with levels of B vitamins, vitamin C, iron, calcium and dietary fibre.

PREPARATION AND COOKING

Although ceps are firm and strong, they are absorbent, so it's best to use a wet cloth to wipe any dirt away and if they are a little on the wet side, wait until they have dried before cleaning. The pores underneath the cap are pretty tightly woven together, so there's not a lot of stuff, including you, that will get in there. Just give the pores a wipe over and they should be fine. Slice widthways, lengthways or into long quarters to cook. If cooking whole, it's best to shave off the end of the mushrooms to check for telltale tiny maggot holes.

Prized in southern Europe, ceps are great in risotto, soups and pasta dishes, but are at their best, simply done, by just grilling them sliced and drizzling with olive oil and sea salt (see the mushroom tapas recipe on page 214). Many chefs have their own special ways of cooking ceps; some say you should never fry them in butter as it brings out a slimy quality, others rave about the almost crystallized effect of ceps fried at length in butter. Some eat them raw and sliced in salads though others say never to eat any wild mushroom raw – probably a sensible notion if you are foraging personally.

Ceps have a certain *je ne sais quoi* when it comes to taste. Sweet, nutty and pleasantly spongy, it's an unmistakable taste that makes you smile if you're a mushroom fan. In this book, we've roasted them whole (page 212), grilled them (page 216), put them in pies (page 202) and baked them in bread rolls (page 140), and are pretty confident they go well in everything!

Good for flavouring risottos and making mushroom stock, dried ceps rehydrate in boiling water in five minutes, leaving rich and flavoursome water behind. Dried ceps can be used as an alternative to fresh mushrooms for some recipes where they are being used for flavour. But dried mushrooms really come into their own when combined with fresh mushrooms, intensifying their flavour and adding a strong brown colour.

Parasol THE FLUFFY ONE

LATIN NAME
Macrolepiota procera

USUALLY FOUND IN
UK, Ireland, Europe, the USA

SEASON
July to November

Storage:
In a plastic container in the refrigerator, the mushrooms will keep for a week, but eat as soon as possible, as this one is delicate.

Nutrition:
Parasols are said to be full of minerals.

Exciting to see growing in the wild, parasols are strong stand-up mushrooms that appear dramatically out of the top of grass from summer to autumn, like little umbrellas. Found in fields, on pathways and in parks, they get their name from their old-fashioned parasol-like fleshy curved cap and thin stem.

Grey, large-capped, rather soft and feathery, parasols grow tall but are actually quite squidgy and delicate once picked. Their tops can be rather shaggy, looking a bit like they have been shredded already. They have a brown tip to the cap in the middle at the top, which gradually breaks down into scale-like skin over a whitey grey underlay. The gills are light and fluffy, with a velvety texture, and has a stipe.

These mushrooms are regularly found in the UK and Ireland, as well as Europe and the USA later in the year, and foragers look for the younger, full-grown mushrooms as parasols are also a favourite of our most prevalent pest, the maggot. Despite their commonness, parasols have failed to catch the imagination in the chef world and are rarely seen on menus.

PREPARATION AND COOKING

Give the parasol a good tap on the top of the cap, over a sheet of kitchen paper, to knock any dirt out of the mushroom's gills. Gently wipe the cap with some slightly wet kitchen paper or clean cloth, then remove the end of the stem. Roast whole drizzled with oil, or grill halved. You can also chop it up and add to stews and soups.

Parasols are popular in Eastern European cuisine, particularly in Poland where they dip it in egg and then breadcrumbs and deep-fried. We prefer them grilled and in stews, and we have also popped them in the mixed mushroom grill (page 216).

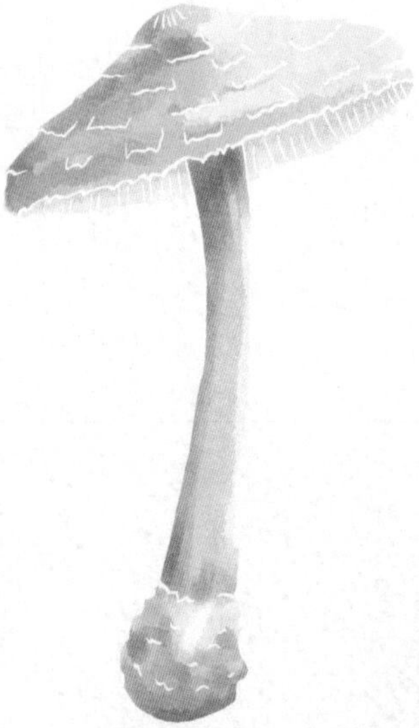

Giant puffball MR BIG

OTHER NAMES
Puffball

LATIN NAME
Calvatia gigantea

USUALLY FOUND IN
UK, Europe, the USA, Central America, Canada

SEASON
August to October

Storage:
Wrap in clear film, plastic wrap or a plastic bag and keep for up to a week in the refrigerator. But, as with all wild mushrooms, eat them as soon as possible to get the best experience and taste.

Nutrition:
Giant puffballs are said to contain calvacin, which can inhibit tumour growth.

Probably one of the most mystical and alluring mushrooms, puffballs are massive feats of nature – an architecturally magnificent fungi. Growing, as if by magic, from tiny strands of mycelium, giant puffballs have no stalk, gills or pores. They are literally large, round balls of mushroom flesh – exciting visually when you find them, but also amazing for the kitchen as you get a bumper portion of that almost porcini-like umami taste without any of the delicate cleaning duties.

Although, like all wild mushrooms, puffballs usually grow in the same place each year, they are only available to buy sporadically through their summer to autumn season. The other reason for their scarcity is because they are often eaten first by cows and other herbivores – puffballs are very much in demand throughout the food chain. They sometimes grow in rings, like mousseron, St George's and pied de mouton, and can be anywhere between 5–12cm/2–4½in wide, and grow to full size in around a week. Commercial foragers look for puffballs after rainfall or when it's been particularly wet, as puffball mycelium likes moist, mostly grassy conditions to grow. As with many mushrooms, puffballs have some poisonous lookalikes, such as the pigskin poison puffball (its surface looks like blistering pigs' skin) or the destroying angel at button stage, so sourcing from a commercial or professional forager is a must.

PREPARATION AND COOKING

When buying giant puffballs, avoid any with yellow staining on them. The yellow indicates that they are old and as soon as you cut them up they will turn the colour of turmeric and become powdery. They can simply be wiped clean with a wet cloth and chopped or sliced. Giant puffballs have a rubbery outside skin that can be peeled but there's no particular reason to do this, especially with young puffballs – there's no real difference between the skin and the consistent, almost marshmallow-like insides. They are brilliant for breakfast, just sliced and grilled, or to use in omelettes. Their texture, although not flavour, has been likened to tofu and they are a dream in tempura batter (see page 186). Like the eryngii, the giant puffball has a firm and thick texture that makes it a good substitute for meat. Basically, we haven't found anything it doesn't go with!

Pied de mouton THE MUSHROOM NEXT DOOR

OTHER NAMES
Hedgehog, the sweet tooth, wood hedgehog

LATIN NAME
Hydnum repandum

USUALLY FOUND IN
UK, Europe, USA, Canada

SEASON
August/September to February

Storage:
Pied de mouton will store for about two weeks, as they are so strong and dry, but again, for quality's sake it's best to eat them as fresh as possible.

Nutrition:
They contain iron, vitamin C, calcium and magnesium.

Multiplying like wildfire in the right conditions and season, the pied de mouton is a commonly found stout, stumpy mushroom which has a meaty off-white or cream-coloured cap with brown highlights. The hefty cap protects its unusual tiny and delicate spines, which flake away from the mushroom at the lightest touch and spread the spores throughout the forest. Another lover of trees, pied de mouton or 'hedgehog' as it is known can be picked throughout Europe, the USA and Canada from early autumn right through to late winter, and is one of the last mushrooms of the season.

The pied de mouton is very distinctive-looking, but its appearance does differ slightly from country to country, depending on its habitat. The Baltic pied de mouton is the first on the market and has a dark yellow or almost orange colour. Then Sweden usually produces a pretty-looking version, with a season in Scotland coming after that. Some have quite a bumpy appearance on the top, while others can have a flatter cap.

Growing in ring formations, like St George's and mousseron, they are relatively easy to find in great numbers. Other members of this family may appear occasionally, but the pied de mouton is the most popular commercially. It has a strong following, mainly in Spain and the USA, and is consistently available throughout its season.

PREPARATION AND COOKING
Pied de mouton is the only widely available and edible mushroom with spines. Thought to be an attribute by some, the spines can spread flavour throughout the dish, but are considered unsightly by others. So, it's up to you, but there are no recipes in this book that ask you to remove the little spines – we think life might be long enough to stuff a mushroom, but probably too short to de-spine pied de mouton...

If you'd like to keep the spines completely intact, however, you do have to be very careful and probably come to terms with the fact that you will lose a few. Take a clean, damp cloth or piece of kitchen roll and, holding the mushroom by the stem, wipe the top, then turn over and wipe the stem, and with a small paintbrush or a pair of tweezers, remove the pieces of dirt. To remove all of the dirt and most of the spines, roughly wipe with the cloth. Slice or use whole.

Often considered a decent substitute for girolles and chanterelles, pied de mouton have a strong taste, a little like mousserons, and a dry texture. They can be peppery and have been likened to oysters and watercress, while some people detect spice and nuttiness. Chefs in the USA use them extensively in stews, soups, sauces, pies and pasta dishes. We have used them mostly as part of a varied wild mushroom mix in a dish, like the roast salmon (page 200) and a partridge stew (page 224), as well as in the fish and mushroom pie (page 198).

Trompette THE BLACK SHEEP

OTHER NAMES
Black trumpet, trumpette, trumpet of death (trompette de mort), black chanterelle

LATIN NAME
Craterellus cornucopioides

USUALLY FOUND IN
UK, Europe, the USA, Canada

SEASON
August to April

Storage:
Trompettes will last a week in the refrigerator from when they are picked, but use them as soon as you wash them as they will break down quickly once wet.

Nutrition:
Trompettes are a good source of vitamin C.

Sprouting out of the forest floors from late summer, dark grey (jet-black when damp) trompettes appear in thin curling funnels in groups around tree bases, lurking in the shadows and waiting to be discovered. A distant cousin of the chanterelle, these are sometimes called the black chanterelle, but are quite different with large hollow, even stems. These mushrooms are hard to spot at first because their colour is very similar to the shade of the forest floor at that time of year, but as soon as a forager eyes them, they can suddenly see them everywhere. Some foragers say that hunting for trompettes is like looking for little black holes in the ground.

As you pull the mushroom out, the long stem is forced from the earth and looks a bit like an old fashioned hearing horn. This managed to give people the rather spooky idea that this was the way that dead people could hear what was going on above ground, and gave the mushroom their name, trumpet of death. Despite the horror stories, these mushrooms are completely edible and have helped form menus throughout Europe from late autumn to winter. They grow in woodlands, particularly under beech and oak trees, throughout Europe, as well as the USA, Japan and Korea.

PREPARATION AND COOKING

Like most wild mushrooms, trompette is time-consuming when it comes to cleaning. These ones grow through the debris, leaving a nice film of mud all over the mushroom. In one of those rare exceptions to the rules, it is probably best, especially if you have a large amount of them, to give trompettes a light bath before endeavouring the big clean. They can hold up to gentle rinsing in lukewarm water, and even drying in a salad spinner. You can then pat them dry with kitchen paper and then rip the larger ones in two and set about wiping them clean. If you have quite a few trompettes, you could now preserve them by drying, spaced out on baking sheets in a hot oven or in direct sunlight. Some say that trompettes take on a truffle taste when dried, so it's definitely worth a go!

In culinary terms, this mushroom is big in both flavour and colour. We have used them in a very autumnal trompette, parsnip and parmesan loaf (page 192), in the batter of our hearty American pancakes (page 190) and to complement some partridge in a stew on page 224, to name a few recipes.

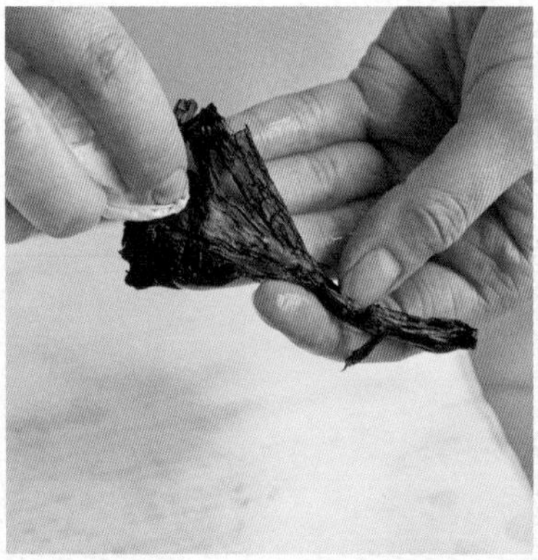

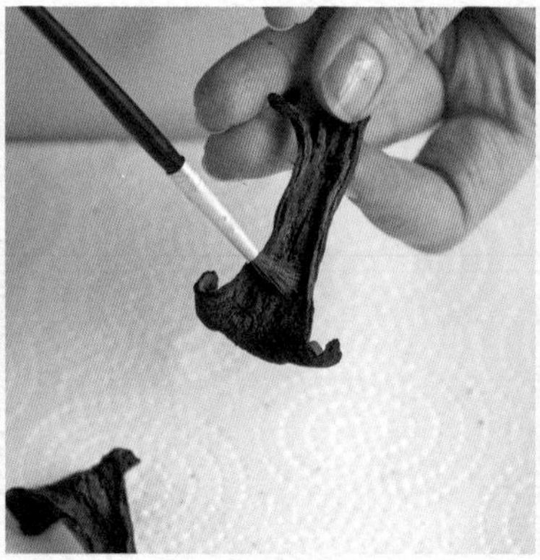

Matsutake THE SACRED ONE

OTHER NAMES
Pine mushroom

LATIN NAMES
Tricholoma matsutake,
Tricholoma nauseosum,
Tricholoma magnivelare

USUALLY FOUND IN
Japan, Asia, USA, parts of Europe

SEASON
September to January

Storage:
Wrap in kitchen paper and keep in the refrigerator. Cook with it as soon as you can to take advantage of its taste, which is better fresh.

Nutrition:
The matsutake is high in protein, with vitamins B and D.

Little known and used in Europe, matsutake is an important and highly sought-after mushroom in Japan, reaching white truffle kind of prices for homegrown. Long and plump, matsutake is also soft and fluffy, with almost a film of cotton-like matter covering it, rather like pied bleu (see page 102). For the best money, the milky white mushroom is picked when the cap has not yet opened and is still curled under the stem. It appears as if there is no divide between the long, thick stem and the pretty, curled-under cap and this illusion continues when sliced. Even before knowing its background, you can tell there's something wonderfully odd about it, as it's very pleasing in texture and taste – it's on the spicy side.

Massively celebrated in Japan, the matsutake is linked to the Japanese symbol for longevity and just as sakura cherry blossom is prized in the spring, the matsutake is an indication of the arrival of autumn and is often given in wooden presentation boxes to celebrate the season or a marriage. That's quite a gift at US$200 for a single mushroom.

A mycorrhizal mushroom, the best matsutake are said to grow in the Japanese region of Tamba at the foot of red pine trees between 20 and 60 years old. The mushroom does, however, also grow throughout Asia, in some places across Europe (mainly Sweden and Finland) and in the USA, where it is also highly thought of. Matsutake grown outside of Japan generate about half as much money, and Japan is the biggest importer of the mushroom. In recent years, a certain bug affecting pine trees in the country has depleted harvests, meaning the price has risen even further.

PREPARATION AND COOKING

For something so worshipped on one side of the world, this mushroom generally turns up pretty dirty and somewhat ugly-looking, usually caked in sandy mud to the end of the stem. They are rather tough and sturdy, and look a bit like a smaller pestle puffball, and can stand being washed in lukewarm water to remove most of the dirt, and even peeled slightly if the debris is stuck. Once the mushroom is clean, remove the very end of the stem and then slice or chop the whole mushroom.

The Japanese say the best way to cook matsutake is to marinade the mushroom in Asian flavours, like soy and fish sauce, then grill or bake. Others pickle the mushroom to preserve its unique spicy or pine-like flavour, or put it in a hot pot. It is good in rice dishes or with chicken or fish, and many recommend placing just one slice into a broth or soup for extra flavour.

We have included it in the pork ramen (on page 206), where it really brings something different to the meal, and in the mushroom tapas (page 214), where you get to taste it very simply done and appreciate its full flavours. If you do manage to get your hands on this mushroom – your best bet is probably in a Japanese supermarket – it's the kind of mushroom that's fun to experiment with it as you would a truffle, using a little here and there.

Cauliflower THE SHOW OFF

OTHER NAMES
The brain fungus, sea sponge, the ruffle mushroom, the white fungus, hanabiratake, sparassis, wood cauliflower

LATIN NAME
Sparassis crispa

USUALLY FOUND IN
Europe, the USA, Canada, Asia, Australasia

SEASON
September to October

Storage:
This is quite a robust mushroom, so it will keep for probably a week or so in the refrigerator. It is also a good mushroom to dry.

Nutrition:
Rather an unusual and clever mushroom, the cauliflower contains antibiotic sparassol and possibly heart disease risk-reducing beta-glucans. It is also thought to strengthen the immune system and repair skin damage. So, very much worth all the cleaning!

Looking more like sea coral than fungi, the cauliflower mushroom, so-nicknamed for its obvious similarities to the vegetable, is frilly, huge and hard to miss. Usually found at the foot of conifer trees throughout Europe, the USA, Canada, Asia and Australasia, the spongy to touch, golden to light cream-coloured fungus is made up of intricate leafy brain-like clusters, a little reminiscent of the springtime morel mushroom's cap, but much larger and with no recognizable stem at all.

Demand for this rather crazy looking mushroom varies from country to country, and whereas it's a rare find in a UK restaurant or market, interest is high in Korea, Japan and the USA, where it is being cultivated for wider use. In the wild, it's mainly an autumn-time special (although seasons do differ between the US states) and when a forager finds it, can be pretty huge, with some reaching a heavyweight 14kg (30lb).

PREPARATION AND COOKING
As you can imagine from its habitat on the forest floor, this mushroom is absolutely riddled with bugs, dirt and leaves, but the good news is that it's very sturdy and almost seaweed-like in its consistency, so it's fine to give it a couple of gentle baths in lukewarm water to get rid of the majority of things you'd rather not eat. After you have washed it, hold the mushroom over a piece of kitchen paper and pat it lightly so more bits fall out, then start ripping it apart and brushing further bits out of it.

After you've got through all that cleaning, it is a great mushroom to cook with. It's used in stews, frittatas, soups and pasta dishes, and it can be braised, roasted, sautéed and fried. We have included it in our tempura mushrooms (page 186), blanched it and combined its nutty texture and taste with a fillet steak on page 210, and paired it with creamy Jerusalem artichokes in a mushroom bake recipe (see page 208).

Lobster THE INVADER

LATIN NAME
Hypomyces lactifluorum

USUALLY FOUND IN
the USA, Canada, Europe

SEASON
September to October

Storage:
If you see them on a farmer's market or a food market, snap them up and cook them as soon as possible as they deteriorate quickly after being picked. Depending on where you buy them, it's most likely they have travelled a few miles to get there, so they will be a couple of days old already.

Nutrition:
Lobster mushrooms are said to contain carbohydrates, protein and fibre.

In a story more suited to science fiction than the pages of a food and cookery book, the way a lobster mushroom grows is akin to an alien invasion out on the forest floor. Technically a parasitic ascomycete fungus, the invading lobster fungus preys on autumn mushrooms, the Russula brevipes and lactaire, and envelopes them in a pimpled red-orange film, coating the gills. This stops the original mushroom from dispelling their spores for future growth and changes its form completely into the concave-cap lobster mushroom.

And, its name isn't random – it's as if some lobster flesh has materialized at the foot of forest trees. This mushroom's uncanny similarity to lobster meat in smell, taste and texture makes for a crazy cooking experience. When cooked the lobster's orange colour weeps out and starts to turn some foodstuffs, like garlic, almost neon green.

Lobster mushrooms really are a bit of a magical mystery tour once you get them in the kitchen, and US chefs, particularly on the east and west coast, eagerly anticipate their season. Because they are so random in where they pop up and troublesome to find, lobster mushrooms can reach £25–£30 (US$40) a kilo, but European chefs are less used to the mushroom, either being fascinated or put off by the fishy lookalike. If you can find lobster mushrooms in Europe, they have probably been imported from the USA, where they mainly grow. The lobster is definitely a mushroom to watch out for – with a short season, interesting appearance and taste, it could be the parasitic fungi *de jour* in the future.

PREPARATION AND COOKING

Lobster mushrooms are covered in what seems like a waterproof film, but unfortunately more often than not they are also caked in mud, so a very quick bath in a bowl of lukewarm to cold water with a clean cloth will get rid of most of the dirt. Then, wipe dry and clean with kitchen paper and either slice or dice, or use whole.

Chefs rejoice in pairing these mushrooms with their lookalike seafood, or in making faux versions of fruits de mer or lobster mushroom benedict. They are good in pasta and grilled simply, and hold up to a fair bit of cooking because they are so sturdy. They pop up a few times in this book, even though availability is comparably low, in case you are lucky enough to find them. Pied de mouton is a good substitute for size and texture or even a large portobello. Take a look at the colourful crab claw terrine (page 172) or baked monkfish stuffed with lobster mushrooms (page 174), or mushroom tapas (page 214) to learn how to cook them simply.

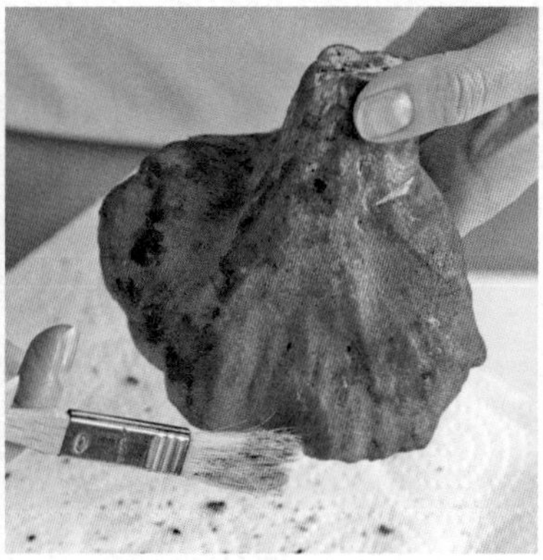

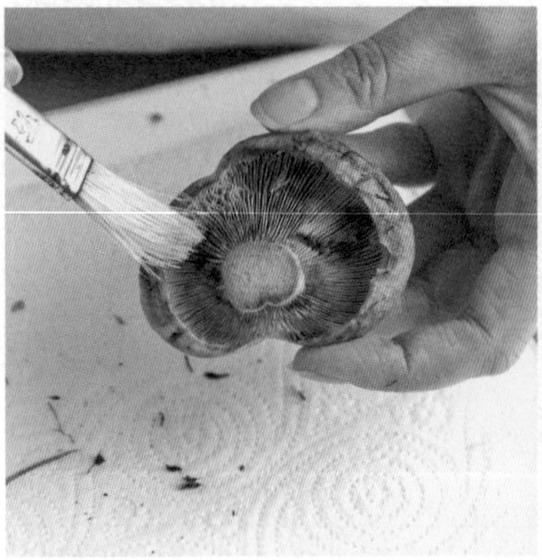

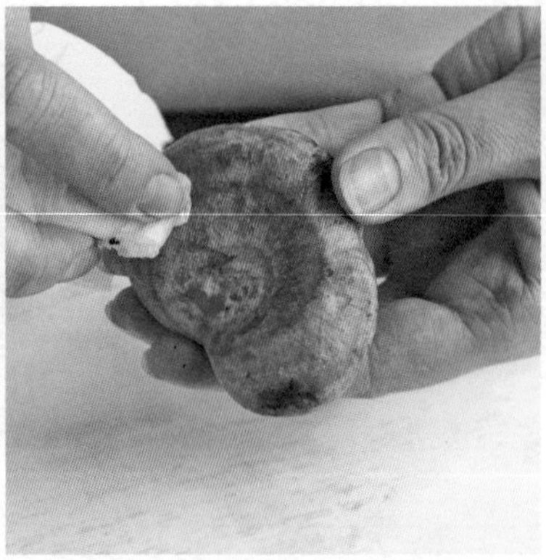

Lactaire THE LOVE IT OR HATE IT MUSHROOM

OTHER NAMES
Milkcap, red pine, saffron milkcap

LATIN NAME
Lactarius deliciosus

USUALLY FOUND IN
UK, Ireland, Europe (particularly Spain, Romania and Turkey), Africa, Central America, Australia, Asia

SEASON
September to October

Storage:
Keep loosely enclosed in a dry paper bag in the refrigerator. If they are damaged or have been cut, eat them as soon as possible as the mushroom will start to deteriorate.

Generally looked upon with love or suspicion, Lactarius is a term that groups many mushrooms belonging to one family. The mushrooms grow mainly in Europe and have brittle, dry gills ranging from yellow to orange, starting to go pinky-purple as they age. As if lactating, the mushrooms also produce a milky fluid when cut, which can discolour – probably one of the main reasons why people are sometimes wary.

Highly regarded in Spain particularly, this discoloured orange flat mushroom has a short season in autumn and sells well on retail markets in that country. There are thought to be other 450 species of this mushroom growing in the northern hemisphere alone. One of the most common lactaires is the woolly milkcap (Lactarius torminosus), which has a creamy colour and grows randomly amongst birch and pine trees throughout the UK and Ireland, Europe, Africa and Asia, however it is poisonous.

PREPARATION AND COOKING
Wipe the tops and stalks of the mushrooms with a clean damp cloth or damp kitchen roll, then brush out any dirt from the gills. Chop or use whole in pasta dishes, stews or simply grilled with oil on toast.

Despite its milky tendency, the mushroom is completely edible, with a dry texture and a flavour that differs from earthy and strong to sweet. We have used the saffron milkcap (Lactarius deliciosus), sometimes known as the red pine mushroom, in the mixed mushroom grill (page 216) and the American-style mushroom pancakes on page 190. Lactarius deliciosus is a popular dish in Catalonia, just fried with garlic and served with fresh parsley, whilst in Poland they are fried in butter, and in Russia they are commonly pickled and served with sour cream.

Truffle THE UNDERGROUND MUSHROOM

OTHER NAMES

The black winter truffle is known as the Périgord truffle; the white truffle is also named the Piedmont White or Alba White

LATIN NAMES

Tuber aestivum (summer black truffle), Tuber melanosporum (black winter truffle), Tuber magnatum (white truffle), Tuber oregonense (Oregon white truffle), Tuber borchii (Bianchetto truffle)

USUALLY FOUND IN

UK, France, Italy, Greece, Spain, Croatia, Romania and Europe in general, Middle East, Africa, USA, Canada, Australia

SEASON

All year, but mostly October to December

In a class and world of its very own, the truffle is a round, hard fungi that grows underground around tree roots. With no stalk, no cap or any real likeness to our usual mushroom friends, its lumpy stone-shaped mass is cut open to reveal a small intricate maze or marbling. The truffle has a romantic mystery to it and has been coveted throughout history, always garnering a high price and even inspiring conflict, whatever the century. Truffles inspire foragers to spend their lives on their hands and knees digging up the earth with specialist tools, hoping that this truffle is going to be a big one.

The age-old gastronomies of France and Italy are famous for both black and white truffles, with English truffle hunters catching on in the 20th century. Hugely popular in the 1900s, truffles were once a mainly peasant food and a village would go out hunting for them and celebrate the season together. Now, they are only really found by people in the know and bought by enthusiasts at sometimes sky-high prices. Most types of truffles are held in high esteem by chefs and in kitchens throughout the world, along with their large sub-category of by-products such as truffle oils, powders, honey and preserves.

Found in woodlands, truffles reproduce via the harvesting process itself, as spore dispersal is achieved through fungivory, which basically means through being moved and eaten. So, even though there are fewer spores about, the more truffles are hunted, the more they could re-appear. Traditional truffle baskets are wicker, allowing the spores to fall out as you carry them. Like mushroom foraging, truffle 'hunting' is a way of life and a serious business. Pigs were used to find the truffles historically, but it was argued that their eagerness to eat the truffle caused more trouble than it was worth, with the possibility that they destroyed important reproducing mycelia in the process. Specialist dogs are now trained to search out the smell, find the spot where the truffle is growing and dig until the hunter says to stop, so they can delicately get the truffle out of the ground without damaging or, most importantly, eating it.

For obvious reasons, the cultivation of truffles or 'trufficulture' has been attempted, again and again, but although there has been some success, it's certainly not to the commercial high standards and volumes of other cultivated mushrooms. Truffle-infected trees can be bought and planted, but it is up to nature whether and when the fungi complies and produces its fruiting bodies – i.e. the truffles. France and Italy have achieved some cultivation in the past, and now there seems to be some success in Australia, where truffles are taking to the soil well, and also in Canada.

> *continues overleaf*

Storage:
Once you buy a truffle, usually in a sealed jar of rice or in a paper bag, it is important to eat it pretty quickly – like any wild mushroom, the fresher the better, but this is particularly the case with truffles. If you leave them in the refrigerator for more than two days, you might miss out on that unique taste – these are words of experience; just eat it! It must stay in the refrigerator and it's best to keep it dry and contained so it doesn't suck up any flavours or moisture. If it becomes immersed in water or liquid, it will become squidgy and pretty useless. It's also a good idea not to prepare or cut it until you use it.

Nutrition:
Truffles generally contain B vitamins, vitamin K and a small amount of vitamin D.

BLACK TRUFFLES

With a season mainly ranging from May to August depending on where you are in the world, black summer truffles are more commonplace in comparison to white or winter black, and although not as pungent, still have an essence of the white truffle taste and a nutty quality. Sizes range in general from 30–100g/1–3½oz, and the taste or strength of the black summer truffle intensifies as they fully mature towards the end of the season. The burgundy truffle (Tuber uncinatum) then takes over, producing from autumn up to December or January. It is similar to its black truffle counterparts, but more pungent and rare. Sometimes called a black Périgord truffle, the winter black type was named after the French region where it is famous for growing and is found from late autumn to early winter.

WHITE TRUFFLES

In general, white truffles are stronger in taste and smell, and are therefore more expensive. There are several different types, with the Italian Piedmont White (Tuber magnatum) and US Oregon White (Tuber oregonense) being very popular. The Piedmont White is indigenous to this northern region of Italy, but is also found throughout Tuscany and Abruzzo, as well as in France, Slovenia and Croatia. An autumn offer, they can grow up to 500g/1lb in size and are picked as low in weight as 10g/¼oz. There are other types of truffle, including the whitish truffle (Tuber borchii), which are lesser known and mostly associated with one area or country.

PREPARATION AND COOKING

To prepare truffles, you first need to remove the mud and dirt on their skin, as they have literally just come from the ground. They shouldn't be washed, so you will need to clean carefully but handle delicately at the same time. If yours is caked with mud (very expensive mud, by the way, so do check over the amount of mud on a truffle before buying), gently tap it with the end of a small paintbrush to remove it and it should flake away. Then with a firm paintbrush or mushroom brush, brush away the dirt, then brush again with a wet paintbrush. If your truffle is still really dirty, it might be an idea to very delicately and sparingly grate around it to get the first brittle coating off, but remember, you are peeling away money. Once you have cleaned your truffle, you can grate or very thinly slice (we recommend using a mandoline or vegetable peeler).

It's best to heat black truffles, even if you are just shaving them for garnish, as cooking brings out the intensity of their flavours. If you are using shavings, you can blanch them in a couple of teaspoons of boiling water, covered, for a few minutes to bring out the aroma and taste. Do use the water as well – it can be added to a stock or sauce, or maybe a different element of the dish.

A good starting point for cooking with truffles is simply shaving the truffle over fried eggs with lots of sea salt, or shaving or grating onto freshly cooked pasta with lots of olive oil. We have used black truffle in a pesto (see roast salmon with truffle pesto on page 200), and to stuff meat or fish, but our favourite recipe with truffle is the simple tapas dish (page 214).

TRUFFLE OIL

Making oil out of truffles is a labour-intensive process, but is one of the best ways to ensure you get all of the flavour for months to come. It takes around two to four weeks to cure the truffles and then the oil has to be infused with the truffles for 24 hours. This is then followed by an ageing process of four to five months before it's ready to use.

Truffle oil is available quite readily in delis and other specialist food shops. You will usually find a white truffle oil, as that's the most pungent. Use the oil very sparingly as a treat in mashed potato or to dress a poached egg on toast, on salads or with pasta or in risotto. A lot of chefs use white truffle oil to give wild or cultivated mushrooms a boost and we have added it to our raw mushroom salad (page 180) to give the shavings of fresh mushrooms a flavour lift. Again, less is more, as this oil can be very overwhelming in both smell and taste, and expensive to waste. You'll also find it garnishing soups (chanterelle and chestnut soup, on page 188), in a truffle aioli with stuffed garlic portobello mushrooms on page 240 and as a flavouring in the trompette, parsnip and Parmesan loaf (page 192). If you have never tried truffles before or are not sure if you like them, then an oil is an inexpensive way to find out more and experiment in the kitchen.

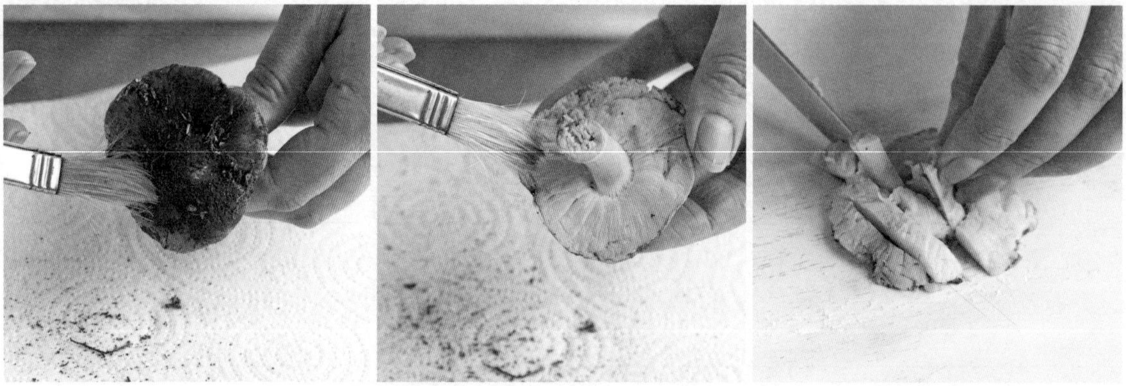

Charbonnier SNOW WHITE

OTHER NAMES
Sooty head

LATIN NAME
Tricholoma portentosum

USUALLY FOUND IN
Europe (mainly Estonia and the Netherlands), the USA

SEASON
October to December

Storage:
These mushrooms can become waterlogged, so keep them dry, in the refrigerator, covered loosely in a paper bag for 2–3 days.

There's not an awful lot known about the mysterious charbonnier and we have rarely managed to get our hands on it. Visually, it's perhaps not as pretty as Snow White but its short, thick stem is as white as snow providing a stark contrast to its black to dark brown sooty, leathery and almost fibrous cap. Its pronounced, lengthy gills are milky-coloured or off-white and this type of mushroom is usually found caked in mud, growing at the base of oak and beech trees. Picked at the right time, after a few days of growth, the charbonnier has a perfectly rounded cap, that just about tucks under at the edges. Larger mushrooms can look a little rough and ready around the cap edge and gills as they are more affected by the elements.

Native to Europe and the USA, charbonnier used to grow quite freely in the Netherlands, but is scarcer there now, although it can now be found in decent numbers in Estonia. Growing from October to December, these mushrooms are relatively large for wild, with caps at about 7.5cm/3in in diameter, and they are soft and fluffy, with a floury and spicy taste and meaty texture. Be careful in identification; there are other members of the Tricholoma family that some advise avoiding due to possible adverse affects.

PREPARATION AND COOKING

First, use a firm brush to remove any debris and dirt from the cap of the mushroom. It will be very dirty, so brush any pieces off onto a piece of kitchen paper. Then take a wet clean cloth or a damp piece of kitchen paper and thoroughly wipe the top. Turn the mushroom over and brush any pieces out of its gills, then trim the stem.

Slice or use whole in omelettes, pasta and soups. Some say charbonnier are particularly good with chicken (see our chicken pot recipe on page 244) and others pickle them.

Wild Agaricus THE ROGUES

ENCOMPASSES
Field mushroom, horse mushroom, the prince

LATIN NAMES
Agaricus campestris, Agaricus arvensis, Agaricus augustus

USUALLY FOUND IN
UK, Ireland, Europe, the USA, Africa, west Asia

SEASON
Summer to autumn

Storage:
Like most wild mushrooms Agaricus should be eaten as soon as possible, or within a week.

We've included this family in both the Wild and Cultivated sections; see page 78 for the cultivated section. There are many kinds of Agaricus species within the genus – the well-known ones found growing wild are field mushroom (Agaricus campestris), horse mushroom (Agaricus arvensis) and the prince (Agaricus augustus), and each differ slightly in taste and looks, from each other and from the Agaricus bisporus. As they grow in the wild, they do tend to have more of a stronger taste, tasting slightly of the matter they grow in, and will be more inconsistent in their appearance. At the moment, they seem to hold little interest to the restaurants or markets in general, but are still highly regarded on the domestic forager's plate.

Field mushroom

Known as either the field mushroom or meadow mushroom, Agaricus campestris has pink gills, a prominent stipe and a mild taste. Saprotrophic, it lives on dead organic matter and appears mostly in fields and in grassy areas after rain. It is a mushroom that grows in rings like the mousserons and pied bleu, and used to be widely found, though it's thought by some foragers that they are not as abundant as they used to be due to modern farming. Said to contain insulin, the field mushroom has been used to dress scalds and burns. As with all wild mushrooms, the field mushroom has its very similar and bad counterpart, the deadly 'destroying angel' (Amanita virosa, Amanita bisporigera in USA) – a cousin of the special and very edible caesar mushroom (see page 44 for details).

The prince

Widespread in the UK, Ireland and Europe, but found only occasionally, the prince (Agaricus augustus) resides in woodlands, growing in groups, and is generally in its largest volumes in August. Tasting of almonds, it contains the same chemical found in sweet almond oil and is called the prince because of its prized aromatic taste. Looking a little similar to the parasol mushroom, the prince can grow to 25cm/10in in diameter, but smaller specimens (about the size of a closed-cup mushroom) are better in taste.

Horse mushroom

The horse mushroom, pictured opposite, starts off life a slight oval but within a couple of days it will open up into the iconic flat mushroom shape. Found in fields and hedgerows from summer into autumn, it has a cap which is a yellowy white, and has a double ring on a white stem. Native to Europe, the UK, the USA, Africa and west Asia, this Agaricus also grows in fairy rings, particularly around nettles, and gets wider and its gills get darker the more mature it gets. Some say it tastes of aniseed or almonds.

CULTIVATED MUSHROOMS

Cultivated Agaricus THE CHAMELEONS

ENCOMPASSES
Button, closed-cup or cremini, giants, flat, chestnut, brown cap, black poplar, portobello, Paris mushroom, Paris white

LATIN NAME
Agaricus bisporus

USUALLY FOUND
They are found everywhere – where people eat mushrooms, this mushroom will be grown commercially

SEASON
Summer to autumn, but available all year

We all know the mushroom Agaricus bisporus very well: these are the mushrooms in your punnets, supermarkets, delis, restaurant and fields. Button mushrooms, closed-cup mushrooms and flat mushrooms are all the same white type of Agaricus bisporus, just at different growing stages (two days, four days and six days, respectively). And it's the same for chestnut mushrooms and portobello mushrooms, which are different sizes of the brown strain. For wild Agaricus see page 74.

With gills varying in colour from pink to grey, and brown to black, and with a ring around their stems, they look like very different mushrooms to the naked eye. Buttons are small, button-sized as you might imagine, and usually very white and smooth on top, with small gills and a perfectly formed cap on a short stem. Closed-cup are around twice the size, with pronounced grey to dark brown gills and a peel or skin that is soft and starting to peel away. Large and spongy, giants are twice as big as the closed-cup and in the process of turning into flat mushrooms, which have opened out, sometimes with the cap's peel still folding over the gills, other times not, and by this time in the growth pattern, the gills are a dark brown to black and the skin is on the grey side, sometimes peeling away in feather-like pieces. Chestnut and portobello mushrooms are the same growth stage as closed-cups and flats, but with a speckled brown colour.

The most popular mushroom for commercial cultivation, Agaricus bisporus grow rapidly but not too quickly to be monitored and stopped, and are easy to produce in the right atmosphere – dark, warmish and moist rather than wet, regulated by state-of-the-art humidity and temperature-control systems. They grow on huge beds of spore-embedded compost, usually in bunk-bed style open shelves.

Traditional commercial cultivation as we know it of the Agaricus bisporus started in the 19th century, although the earliest record of this mushroom's cultivation dates back to 1650, in a French back garden. By the late 1800s, mushrooms were being grown in caves in many parts of France and Britain, 30 metres (100 feet) below the ground. Darkened candlelit rooms housed rows of mycelium-enriched soil in damp, naturally air-conditioned conditions – just right for mushrooms to grow. They produced the 'Paris mushroom' or 'Paris white', which was basically the same as our button mushroom today, but pulled from the ground rather than cut short, with some romantic dirt still attached to the stem.

> *continues overleaf*

Agaricus mushrooms, clockwise from top: portobello, chestnut, flat, button and horse mushrooms >

Storage:
Keep uncovered in plastic punnets in the refrigerator and use within a week or as soon as possible.

Nutrition:
Containing C, B2, B3 and B5 vitamins, as well as some vitamin D.

As technology and demand increased, The Netherlands became the place to grow mushrooms around the 1970s. The country's first above-ground mushroom cultivating facility was built in 1950 and The Netherlands continues to be the largest mushroom producer in Europe, with its main mushroom being Agaricus bisporus in all its modern forms. Through time, cultivation trays have been concrete, been lined with wooden boxes and then changed to wooden beds, but today mechanized metal trays are used. Other European countries have also seen the economic and gastronomic advantages of cultivating mushrooms in great numbers, like Ireland, Belgium, Britain and Poland, to name a few.

It's hard to estimate the amount of Agaricus bisporus that's cultivated in the world. West to East, all sizes of the white and brown mushrooms are eaten on a daily basis. They are a staple in almost every professional kitchen and most domestic kitchens.

PREPARATION AND COOKING

As they have been grown in such a controlled and clean environment, button, chestnut, closed-cup, flat and portobello mushrooms can be just brushed gently to remove any dirt with a pastry brush or a dry piece of kitchen paper. Wipe the top of the cap, gills and the stem with some dry kitchen paper to remove any dirt or marks.

Some peel Agaricus bisporus to make sure they are extra clean or for a better texture, and others show off their knife skills by fluting the tops, but mostly people just slice, dice or cook whole.

These mushrooms are used all over the world in curries, stews, omelettes, soups, stir-fries, risottos, raw in salads, cooked in garlic butter, and so much more. You can use these mushrooms as a replacement for any of the more exotic cultivated mushrooms used in the recipes of this book. Obviously certain tastes and textures will differ, but as long as you cut them up to emulate the shape of the mushroom in the recipe it will work.

Cooked, these mushrooms generally soak up the flavour of the dish they are in, but raw, button mushrooms in particular can taste like coconut, and the chestnut mushrooms, like a chestnut! The Agaricus bisporus has that umami taste so associated with mushrooms and adds texture and zing to any meal.

Chestnut mushrooms >

Button mushroom

The smallest stage of the Agaricus bisporus mushrooms, the button is usually around 5cm/2in in width, and as neat and small as its namesake. Some growers are now producing mini buttons, weighing in at about 8g each, but this isn't widespread at the moment. The original Paris mushroom or Paris white, buttons grown in professional facilities are picked before they can become bigger and end up as closed-cup or flat mushrooms.

Widely popular in the Western world, button mushrooms are perfect baked in garlic butter (what isn't), in a traditional English breakfast or sliced on a pizza. We have preserved them with some of spring's wild mushrooms in our mushrooms in oil recipe on page 142, added them to our fish and mushroom pie (with many twists) on page 198, and they are one of the gang of mushrooms thinly shaved and presented as a raw mushroom salad (see page 180). Button mushrooms are especially useful if you can't find one of the smaller wild mushrooms in the shops, and provide a good alternative to mushrooms like pied bleu or horse.

Flat mushroom

Flat mushrooms are the largest of the white strain of Agaricus bisporus and, of the mushrooms cultivated in substrate, are the closest to the wild field mushrooms. With brown to red-brown or black large gills and firm thick white to grey caps, they grow to the size of your palm, with the larger ones opening out completely to reveal thin edges, rather than the caps curling over the gills.

A really meaty mushroom in texture, flat mushrooms are great as a vegetarian main, whole with a stuffing or topping, and a tasty, chunky addition chopped up in a stew or soup. To clean, tap the cap of the mushroom, holding the mushroom gills down so any dirt drops out, then wipe the cap with a damp piece of kitchen roll. We have used flat mushrooms throughout the book, and again, they are great as a wild alternative, if you need a more substantial mushroom replacement. We have stuffed them with garlic breadcrumbs and topped the dish with a truffle aioli on page 240.

Portobello mushroom

The very popular portobello mushroom, sometimes just known as the portobello, is pretty similar to the flat mushroom in size and texture, but has a brown, almost speckled colour to its cap. The skin across the cap also separates and breaks, giving the look of hen feathers. In addition to the substantial amount of vitamin D Agaricus bisporus contain, portobello mushrooms also have high amounts of copper and selenium.

The portobello mushroom is considered the most mature of the Agaricus mushrooms and it has a slightly stronger taste than the flat mushroom. They have provided that extra mushroom taste in our creamy mixed mushroom and tarragon soup recipe (page 148) and are a good alternative to hen of the woods if you can't find any. Clean portobello mushrooms in the same way you would flat mushrooms (see page 83).

Chestnut mushroom

The middle-sized brown strain of Agaricus bisporus, chestnut are the same size as closed-cup, with the colour and sometimes feather-like pattern of portobello. Also known as brown cap or black poplar in the USA, they have a stronger taste than the white Agaricus bisporus; some say like chestnuts, others believe they were named chestnut because of their tanned appearance. They are common in Europe and Asia, and are also sometimes know as baby portobello.

To prepare, wipe the tops and stalks with damp kitchen paper, then use whole, or slice or quarter. Chestnut mushrooms can be eaten raw – you can add them to the mix in our raw mushroom salad on page 180 – and are used in breakfasts, in stews or casseroles, soups and many more dishes. Check out the springtime tarts on page 134, which can be made at any time of the year by adding more chestnut mushrooms when mousserons aren't available.

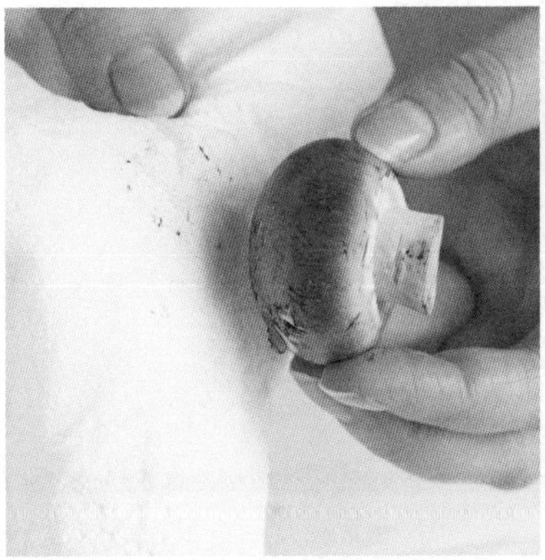

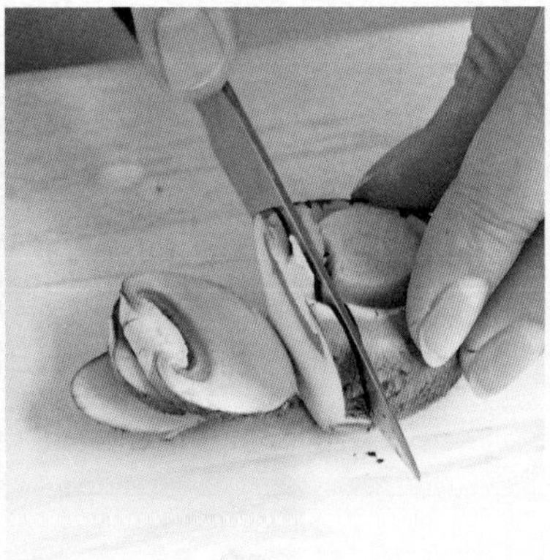

Oyster THE TREE LOVER

OTHER NAMES
Grey oyster, tree oyster, hiratake (in Japan), the vegetarian steak, tamogitake, dhingri, oyster shelf

LATIN NAMES
Pleurotus ostreatus, Pleurotus cornucopiae

USUALLY FOUND IN
The world over

SEASON
Spring to winter, but available all year

Nearly as rich in diversity as the Agaricus (see page 78), the Pleurotus genus encompass delicate fan-like mushrooms of many different colours and sizes, of which there are at least four we regularly enjoy eating. Commercially cultivated and plentifully available, this includes the grey or silver oyster (Pleurotus ostreatus), the smaller bright-yellow golden oyster (Pleurotus cornucopiae var citrinopileatus), the pale rose-coloured pink oyster (Pleurotus djamor) and the larger eryngii (Pleurotus eryngii – see page 100 for more details on this one).

Full bodied and delicate, the oyster mushroom is the most like an old-fashioned lady's fan, with light-coloured gills starting from the tip of the cap to the base of the mushroom, where there is a slight stem. Light and almost spongy in texture, the cap is velvety and usually slightly darker grey than the gills.

The golden oyster mushroom – named tamogitake in Japan – grows in clusters with long stems and small, round trumpet-like caps. They are bright yellow to golden brown with a velvety, dry surface texture and looks similar to the winter chanterelle (page 40).

The pink oyster mushroom grows more like the original oyster in ear shapes, coming away in a fan from the chosen decaying wood or tree in the wild or growing substrate in a growing tunnel. As you might expect, this oyster ranges from light pink to hot pink and can grow as large as the main oyster mushroom, although it is often grows to about half the size.

Being saprophytic and extremely versatile in different conditions, the wild oyster mushroom grows everywhere and anywhere in both temperate and tropical forests from Europe to Asia, the US and the UK, on dying trees, especially beech, and decaying wood. It is a 'carnivorous' mushroom and attracts nematode worms towards it so the nitrogen can be sucked out of them.

Pretty much able to survive all kinds of atmospheres, oyster mushrooms are big business in the cultivated world and have been encouraged to grow for centuries on logs or tree stumps in Asia, much the same way as shiitake mushrooms are and have been. Oyster mushrooms are now typically grown in substrate blocks coated in plastic within professional facilities and are the third most-produced mushroom by volume in Asia.

> *continues overleaf*

Golden oyster mushrooms >

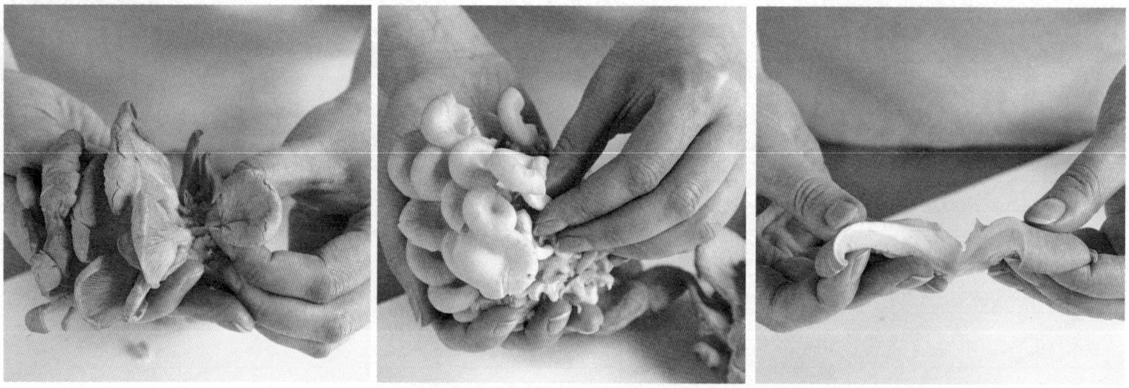

Storage:
Keep in the refrigerator in a plastic container, uncovered. They can last up to 2 weeks, but they do dry out, so like all mushrooms eat them as soon as you can.

Nutrition:
Full to the brim with good stuff, oyster mushrooms are high in protein, fibre and iron, with levels of zinc, potassium, niacin, selenium, calcium, phosphorus, folic acid and vitamin C and D, as well as antioxidants. It has also been found that they contain antihyperglycemic properties, which decrease blood sugar levels, as well as containing the cholesterol-lowering drug, lovastatin.

PREPARATION AND COOKING

Break away the oyster mushrooms from the stem base or each other, cutting off any tough parts that the mushrooms have grown from. The majority of the oyster mushrooms we eat will be cultivated and as a result are grown in very clean conditions, not touching any compost once they grow. A swift wipe with a piece of damp kitchen paper will suffice, as they are very delicate. The smaller oysters, especially the pink and golden, can stay whole to cook, and even the standard oysters can be griddled whole for that 'vegetarian steak' effect. Otherwise, it's best just to tear oyster mushrooms from the top to the bottom into strips or smaller pieces.

A big part of Asian cookery, oyster mushrooms are sometimes used as a replacement for or like a protein, holding their shape through gentle stir-frying, in soups and sauces. Some say they taste of coconut, others think they are more like almonds, as they contain the aromatic compound benzaldehyde that's also in the nut. But, like a lot of mushrooms, it is the oyster mushroom's delicate, yet robust texture that turns heads when it comes to cookery.

We have added them to our traditional Chinese mushroom curry on page 230 and the Chinese broth (page 250), but also diversified by adding pink and yellow oysters to the rare beef and mushroom open sandwich on page 226, and made them the star of the show in a delicate and tangy mushroom ceviche (page 150).

Shiitake THE WISE ONE

OTHER NAMES
Black mushroom, hua gu, the Japanese mushroom, fragrant mushroom

LATIN NAME
Lentinus edodes

USUALLY FOUND IN
Japan, China, South Korea, the USA, Russia, Holland, UK

SEASON
All year

Storage:
Keep the fresh mushrooms in a refrigerator in a loose container, away from anything wet. Dried shiitake should be kept in a sealed container in a cool cupboard.

Nutrition:
Contains iron, vitamin B and D and zinc.

One of the most popular mushrooms in the world, shiitake have always been as prevalent and important to Eastern food culture as the closed-cup mushroom is to the West. They stand out from the mushroom crowd in many ways, as they are hardy and textured, with almost tiger-like markings when they start to dry, and are full of their own unique 'umami' flavour. As well as tasting good, these chewy fungi aid our immune and cardiovascular systems; a super-healthy mushroom, they have been used in Chinese medicine for centuries.

The traditional wooden bark method of growing shiitake encourages larger volumes of the mushroom by extending its growing environment, and this was the sole way of growing shiitake until the early 1980s, when factory cultivation came into play. Although the traditional methods are still widely used in the mushroom's natural habitat of Japan, China and South Korea, in Europe shiitakes are mostly grown in substrate blocks in darkened, damp rooms.

There are two main methods of production; the mushroom spores are grown in substrate blocks, such as a mix of wheat, straw, bran and oak sawdust, or on wooden bark or logs. The perfect environment for shiitake mushrooms to grow is around 18°C, with a flow of fresh air and a constant water mist. Shiitake grow, like most cultivated mushrooms, in flushes, which produce a certain amount of crop, and you get about three flushes per substrate block. To stress the shiitake mycelium into producing more fruit (i.e. mushrooms), the substrate blocks are beaten with a stick-like instrument in between growing flushes one and two. With the right conditions, it takes 10 to 14 days to grow a crop of shiitake – quite a lengthy time in the mushroom world.

Shiitake mushrooms can be bought fresh and semi-dried. You will find that young shiitake mushrooms are softer, more delicate in flavour and pale brown, whereas semi-dried mushrooms are creamy brown with patches of dark brown, sometimes like tiger markings, and with more of a strong traditional shiitake flavour. Shiitakes grown closer to home will be picked fresh and transported straightaway, but the most common type, the East Asian shiitake, is semi-dried for around three days ahead of a longer journey to its destination market. They are also sold fully dried, and sometimes pickled.

PREPARATION AND COOKING

Widely used in Asian cooking, shiitake mushrooms are common in soups (miso mainly), noodle dishes and with oyster sauce, and need a little more cooking then the average mushroom as they are quite sturdy. They are great in stocks as, unlike a lot of mushrooms, they have a strong, distinct flavour. Their texture and taste make them a good meat substitute.

To clean, take some damp kitchen roll and delicately dab any dirt or stains from the top of the cap and stalk. Then with a clean, dry pastry brush, gently brush away any dust or dirt. If the stalk is woody, trim the end. Do not wash these ones, as they absorb moisture like a sponge.

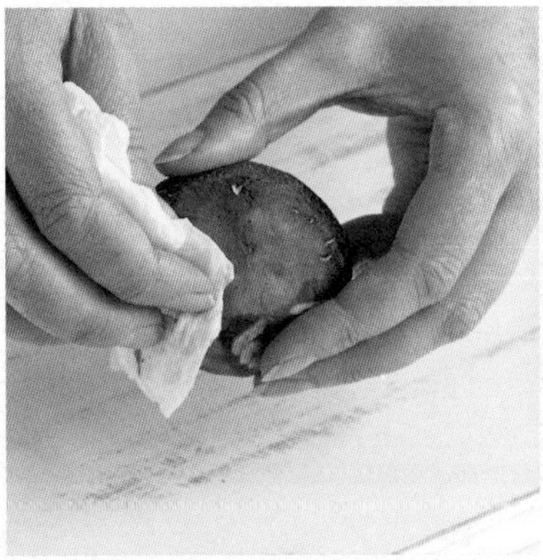

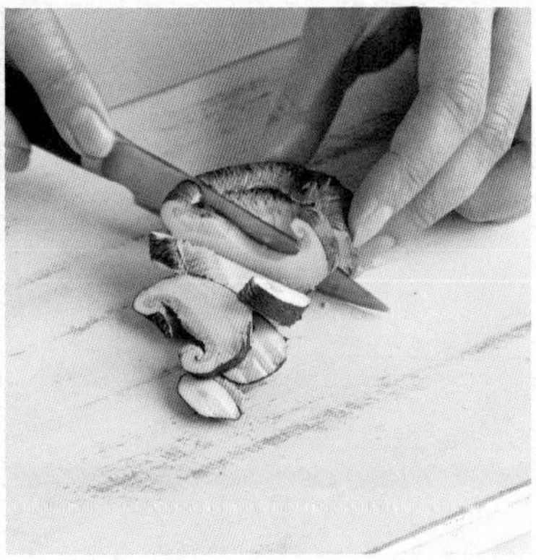

Enoki and golden enoki THE FUNGI NOODLE

OTHER NAMES
Enokitake, enokidake, seafood mushroom, winter mushroom, winter fungus, velvet foot, golden needle mushroom, lily mushroom, nameake, snow puff mushroom

LATIN NAME
Flammulina velutipes

USUALLY FOUND IN
Japan, South Korea, China, Thailand, UK, the Netherlands, the USA

SEASON
September to March, but available all year

Like natural spindly and bright micro-fibers, enoki grows in long, thin, off-white stems round 30cm/12in with pinhead-sized tiny caps. Enoki's mushroom cap features are so small, that you have to look very closely to even realize it's a fungus. Delicate in texture, with a squidgy bite, enoki has a sweet, almost sesame seed oil taste and makes for a great noodle or pasta alternative.

Whilst most cultivated mushrooms bear similarities to the wild fungus they are derived from, the cultivated and wild versions of enoki are strikingly different to each other. A saprotroph, the wild enoki grows out of tree bark and naturally grows to the size of closed-cup mushrooms with a yellow to orange-gold hue, compared to its more neat and willowy cultivated counterpart.

Amazingly versatile, this mushroom has been known to survive a frost while fruiting, with the mushrooms literally freezing, thawing and then continuing to grow, making it the perfect specimen for cultivation. It is said that this variety has been cultivated on logs in Japan for more than 300 years. Today, in commercial growing facilities, the white enoki grows from substrate in bottles, completely in the dark. Chilled growing conditions with a high level of carbon dioxide makes the fruiting mushroom strive for light and oxygen, resulting in long, thin mushrooms with tiny features. Growing from substrate in uniform flushes, the mushroom is sold in same-weight clumps, still partially attached to its growing matter; they are pulled out of the jar, making them very easy to harvest. They are harvested just before the gills mature, meaning that they have extremely good shelf life.

> *continues overleaf*

Storage:
Kept in their packaging, enoki can last in the refrigerator for up to two weeks, but once you cut it from its substrate, use it straight away.

Nutrition:
Rich in an amino acid and antioxidants, enoki is thought to be anti-cancerous and contains a decent level of protein. It is used in Chinese medicine and believed to cure certain liver diseases and stomach ulcers. Enoki also contains vitamin B, potassium, magnesium, iron and a small amount of vitamin D.

You can also get a golden enoki, which is a shorter version of the white cultivated enoki mushroom, but which has golden-brown caps and golden-yellow stems, much like the wild Flammulina velutipes. Grown in plastic bags or jars, golden enoki comes in a punnet and smells of slightly overripe fruit. Also called 'golden needles', the caps are moist to eat and, when cut off their stems, make convincing mushroom 'caviar'.

PREPARATION AND COOKING

Give the mushrooms a rinse in running cold water, then cut them away from the end of the substrate. They are now ready to use, although some cooks dice them into smaller pieces. Brilliant to use in place of noodles and good with fish or in soups or stir-fries, enoki and golden enoki are used extensively in Japanese, Chinese, Vietnamese and Korean cooking. They are particularly known for their role in the Japanese hot pot sukiyaki.

Enoki can be eaten raw in salads or blanched quickly to soften slightly. We have used them blanched in our take on Thai salad (page 168), and raw in the mushroom sushi recipe on page 162. We have also included enoki in an Asian mushroom and pork ramen, and Chinese broth (see pages 206 and 250 for the recipes), as well as for some more unusual combinations in mushroom piccalilli (page 176) and Japanese sweet golden enoki green tea buns on page 232, to name a few.

Golden enoki mushrooms >

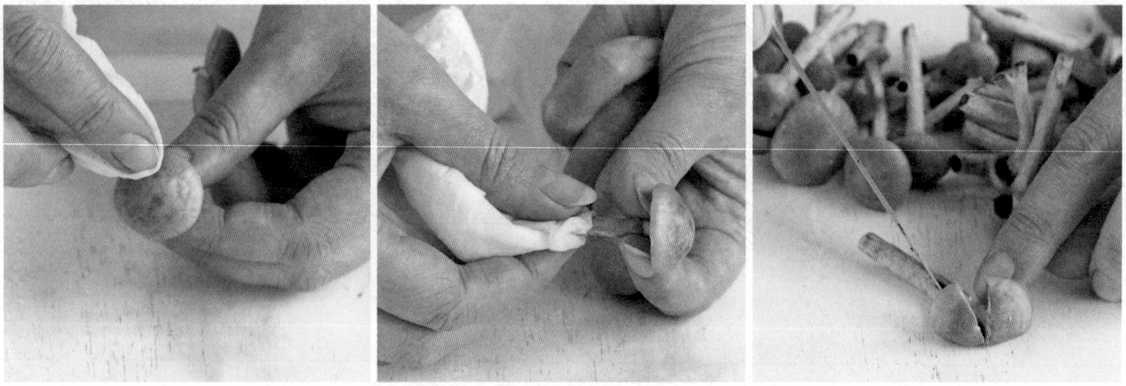

Nameko THE LITTLE JELLY

OTHER NAMES
Butterscotch mushroom

LATIN NAME
Pholiota nameko

USUALLY FOUND IN
Asia, especially Japan and China

SEASON
November to February, but available all year

Storage:
Store in open containers in the refrigerator for up to two weeks.

Nutrition:
Nameko contains calcium, potassium, sodium, and a lot of the B vitamins.

This mostly cultivated mushroom, nameko looks like a mix between shimeji and golden enoki and is considered a gourmet mushroom in Asia. The toadstool lookalike has been reproduced on substrate blocks in plastic bags by Japanese companies for the last 10 years or so, but was originally cultivated on logs. Forming 21 days after the substrate is inoculated, it then swiftly grows to full size amid monitored conditions in two to three days. It is indigenous to temperate forests in Asia and grows naturally on hardwood stumps and logs, making it a good decomposer, like our friend the oyster.

Also known as the 'butterscotch mushroom' in the US and popular in Russia, its honey-coloured caps have a jelly-like film when raw, which disappears when cooked. Nameko is good in Asian soups, hot pots and stir-fries, and is sticky and nutty in taste. We have used this attractive looking mushroom in our ramen recipe on page 206.

Shimeji THE BRANDED ONE

OTHER NAMES
Beech, elm oyster, mountain echo mushroom

LATIN NAME
Hypsizygus tessellatus

USUALLY FOUND IN
Asia, Europe, North America, Australia

SEASON
Autumn, but available all year

Storage:
Store in open containers in the refrigerator for up to two weeks.

Nutrition:
Rich in dietary fibre, shimeji contains antioxidants, niacin, vitamins and minerals.

Shimeji is a small, firm white or brown mushroom with a both crunchy and chewy texture and somewhat of a cult following in Asia. So perfectly formed they almost look cartoon-like, shimeji comes in both white, otherwise known as bunapi-shimeji, or brown (known as buna-shimeji), and it is grown under brand names throughout Asia. Firm and fragrant, these mushrooms are also called brown shimeji and white shimeji, and in Japan, they are generally believed to be the tastiest mushrooms you can get. The white shimeji is brilliant white with perfectly formed caps the size of the tip of your thumb, whereas the brown shimeji has identical white stems but with light brown caps featuring a darker brown almost dried marble effect.

Over the years, the term 'shimeji' has become an umbrella name for around 20 different shimeji mushroom species, but in the Western world it is most commonly known as the beech mushroom. They lend themselves well to commercial cultivation, reaching extreme high standards of quality and are usually cultivated in sterilized bottles or jars of substrate, in controlled growing rooms at a temperature of around 14°C and with a humidity level of 80%.

Like any mushroom that's been coaxed to grow from its wild spores in an artificial environment, its form is ever so slightly different to its wild original, which can be found growing in great numbers throughout Asia, America and Australia. Growing in clusters, they do well in hotter climates, but wild grow throughout the world. Native to East Asia and found growing naturally on beech trees, hence the name, the mushrooms have a long stem in portion to their smooth cap, so small that the gills are invisible to the naked eye.

PREPARATION AND COOKING

These cultivated mushrooms are quite sturdy and self-contained, so can handle a swift rinse under cold running water before you prepare them. Once washed, simply cut off the substrate bottom and either blanch to use in a salad, stir-fry or add to a soup or sauce. Although edible raw, they have a slightly bitter essence, and mostly people tend to cook them. Keeping its firm yet squidgy texture when cooked, this mushroom has a sweet, nutty taste and is known for its inclusion in the Japanese rice dish 'takikomi goham'.

Highly regarded as a gourmet mushroom in Japan, shimeji naturally features in many of our Asian influenced recipes like mushroom sushi, Asian mushroom and pork ramen, and som tum (pages 162, 206 and 168), but we have also experimented with its taste and textures for the less-traditional recipes morel and shimeji flatbreads (page 136) and the mushroom pork pie (page 154).

Eryngii THE KING OF CULTIVATED

OTHER NAMES
King oyster, king trumpet, French horn mushroom

LATIN NAME
Pleurotus eryngii

USUALLY FOUND IN
South Korea, Japan, Taiwan, China, Italy, the USA, the Netherlands, Germany, Spain

SEASON
Autumn, but available all year

Storage:
They can keep in the refrigerator, in a plastic container away from anything wet, for up to 2 weeks.

Nutrition:
The eryngii is said to be good for the immune system and contains compounds that lower cholesterol.

Nicknamed the king oyster, the eryngii is just that – a long, mighty thick mushroom, looking like but far sturdier than a cep, with a solid stem that turns into a slightly gilled top, reminiscent of an oyster mushroom. Growing wild from the Mediterranean to Asia, the king oyster is quite different to its saprotrophic cousin, the oyster, as it grows as a parasitic fungi on the roots of plants. Cultivated in Asia in worldwide commercial volumes since the early 1990s, eryngii's popularity is gaining worldwide, as it proves to be a very versatile ingredient in the kitchen. Due to their similarity to ceps in appearance, if not flavour, eryngii are a favourite with chefs, particularly when the bulk of other wild mushrooms are out of season, and are a consistent ingredient in Asian restaurants.

The cultivated eryngii is always of a consistent quality and there's a constant supply. Grown in either jars or plastic bags of sterilized substrates of sawdust and bran, eryngii are generally grown in an automated system, which adds water at the right time and allows in much-needed air. The jars or bags spend six weeks incubating at 20°C and then, amid a humidity of 99%, harvesting can start three weeks later. Possessing an amazing shelf life, eryngii travels for three weeks, packed in airtight packaging in temperature-controlled chambers of boats from Asia to get to Europe, and then they can last up to two weeks after that in the refrigerator.

PREPARATION AND COOKING

Wipe with a piece of damp kitchen paper, before cutting away the ends if they are a little dry, and either leave whole or slice vertically or horizontally. Slightly sweet-tasting, eryngii are one of the mushrooms with a good umami taste and a soft yet firm, sponge-like texture that soaks up flavours. Its stem is similar to a giant puffball and can be chopped and fried, and added to a whole host of dishes from breakfast to stews, and its cap can be used like an oyster mushroom. However it does seem a shame not to make the most of this mushroom's full and impressive stature: it is great halved, hollowed out and stuffed (see our stuffed eryngii using crab on page 160) or sliced and griddled on the gourmet mushroom burger (on page 170). They are also a great alternative to fish or meat, and we slice them into cylinder shapes in the way of faux scallops, fry in butter and brandy, then pair with lobster and cream on page 158.

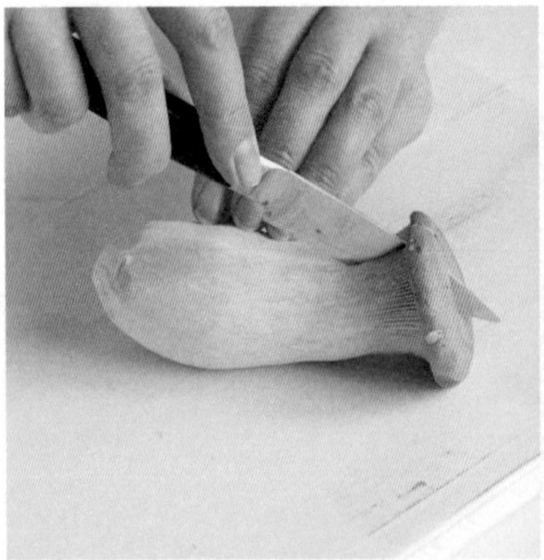

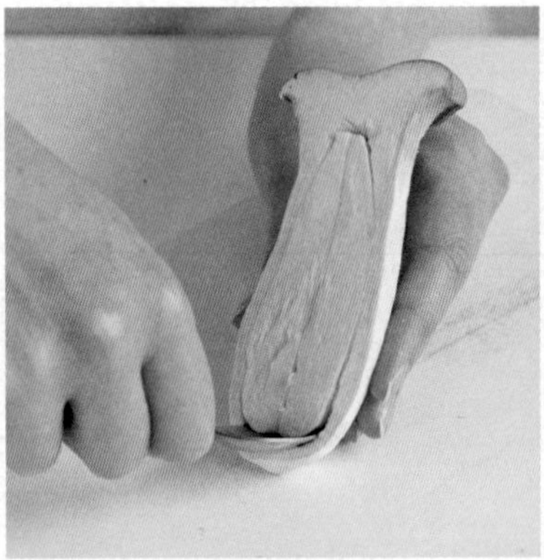

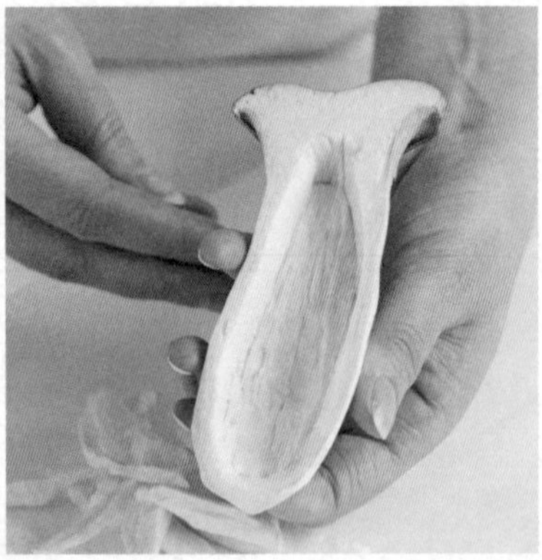

Pied bleu THE CAVE DWELLER

OTHER NAMES
Field blewit, blewit, blue stalk mushroom, the blue foot, rhodopaxille nu, blue leg

LATIN NAME
Lepista saeva

USUALLY FOUND IN
Europe (in particular France, the UK, the Netherlands and Hungary), the USA

SEASON
October to January, but available all year

Things of visual wonder, pied bleu are small with dark purple stems and light blue caps. They grow slowly but surely amid a soft, silky layer of wispy white web in fairy ring formations on the forest floor. Like something out of science fiction, the weave of insulating natural material, rather like a blend of a spider's web and cotton wool in texture, almost cocoons the mushrooms, protecting them from cold temperatures as autumn changes to winter.

A distant cousin of St George's mushroom (see page 30), another saprotrophic mushroom that grows in circles on decaying leaves and matter, the pied bleu differs in form according to whether it is wild or cultivated. The wild pied bleu has a dirty brown cap, a bluish-lilac stem and gills that are whitish to flesh-coloured, whilst the cultivated type has a purple-blue hue or tint rather than a full colour. A stout little mushroom about twice the height of the button mushroom, it has a sturdy, solid almost chalky stem. A great offer throughout the year for chefs looking for something a bit unusual for their menus, they tend to stick to the cultivated version because of its consistently good quality and, consequently, there is less demand for the wild in autumn as there are so many other wild mushrooms about to choose from.

Growing seasonally in the wild from autumn to winter, the wild version can get quite large and flimsy. It's generally wetter and prone to maggots, whereas the cultivated types are particularly sturdy and robust in cooking. Both the wild and cultivated pied bleu have a strong woody smell and taste, some describing it as fruity.

We have used pied bleu quite a lot in this book, as they really help pad out the gaps in the year where you don't have many wild mushrooms – and although this mushroom is cultivated, it appears and cooks like a wild mushroom, making it invaluable for wild mushroom lovers and chefs.

> *continues overleaf*

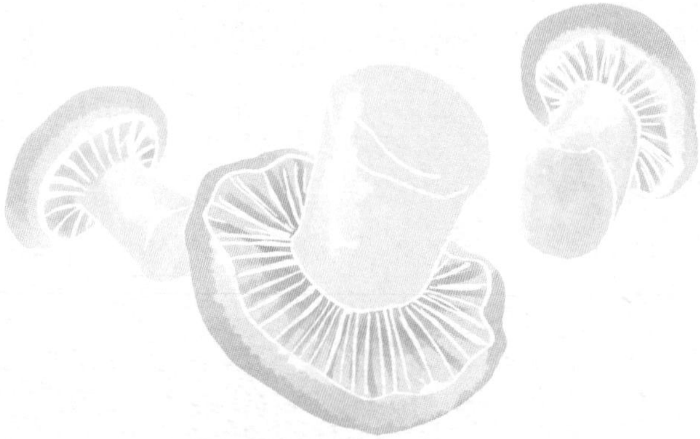

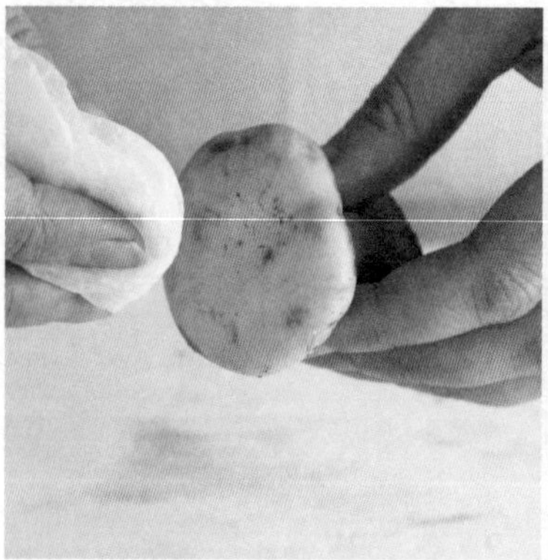

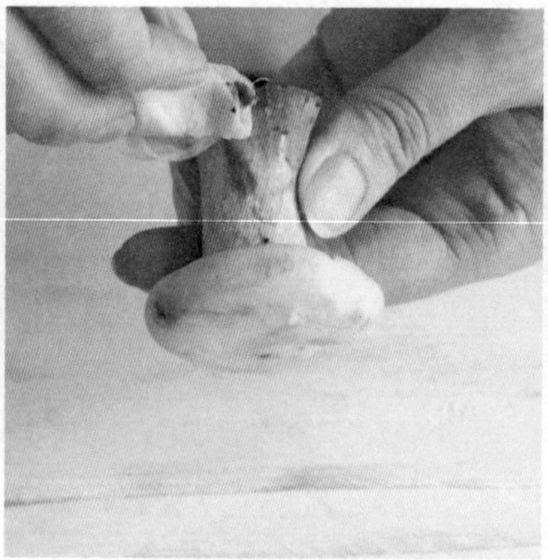

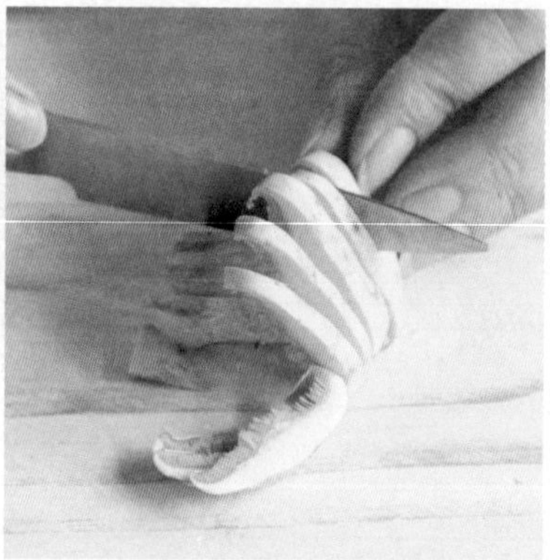

Storage:
Cultivated pied bleu are strong and robust, so will last a week at least in the refrigerator. Keep them uncovered and in a plastic container. As mentioned, the wild version of this mushroom can be very waterlogged, so it is best to eat it as fresh as possible. You can store it in the same way, but the sooner it is used, the better. The insulating web will continue to grow in the refrigerator with time and can make the mushrooms become unpleasant and damp.

Nutrition:
Thought to help support the nervous system, pied bleu contain decent levels of vitamin B1 and D, and high levels of carbohydrates.

PREPARATION AND COOKING

Because of their sometimes fuzzy film of white web, it is a good idea to take a wet cloth or damp kitchen roll to the stem of pied bleu mushrooms, moving the cloth downwards in a stroking motion to remove the web, as well as any dirt. The gills are usually quite close together and therefore clean, but it is probably worth investigating with a small brush. Gently rub the cap of the mushroom with the cloth to remove any dirt then slice, halve or cook whole.

A stronger-tasting mushroom with a firm texture, pied bleu is usually paired with big flavours and sturdier foods such as seafood, sweetbreads, onions, garlic and chives, as well as other strong-tasting fresh herbs. The pied bleu's robust nature makes it a great addition to a jar of preserved mushrooms in oil (see page 142) and we also include them in the mushroom pork pie on page 154. They give texture to pâté (page 218) and are used whole for flavour and texture in our chicken in a pot recipe on page 244.

The wild version of pied bleu has been known to cause allergic reactions in some, and it shouldn't be eaten raw.

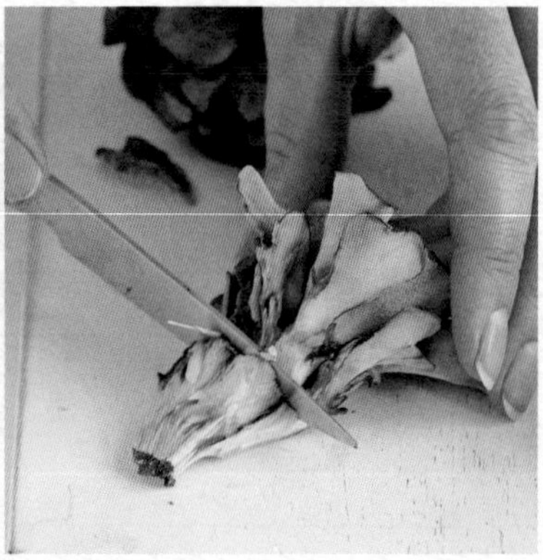

Maitake TINY DANCERS

OTHER NAMES
Hen of the woods, dancing mushroom, cloud mushroom, dancing butterfly, signorina

LATIN NAME
Grifola frondosa

USUALLY FOUND IN
Asia, the USA, UK, Europe

SEASON
Autumn, but available all year

Storage:
Store in open containers in the refrigerator for up to two weeks.

Nutrition:
Not just a tasty addition to our mealtimes, this is the first mushroom to be confirmed to have anti-HIV properties, and it contains both vitamin D and B6.

Considered a delicacy, this cultivated version of the wild Hen of the Woods forms in clusters of multiple grey feather-like thin caps, with no real stem or gills, which can be scattered like flower petals in dishes. This light, pretty mushroom is a polypore and has tiny pores on the underside of the caps.

Maitake is parasitic and so grows at the base of living oak and beech trees. Like a good deal of the Asian cultivated mushrooms, its spores are transferred to sterile jars or bottles and grown in monitored factory-like conditions in abundance. Tasting nutty and fruity, maitake are used in the full repertoire of Asian dishes. We have added them to our chicken in a pot recipe (see page 244) and the ramen dish on page 206.

Straw THE MINI

OTHER NAMES
Paddy straw mushrooms

LATIN NAME
Volvariella volvacea

USUALLY FOUND IN
Hong Kong, Thailand, Taiwan, Indonesia

SEASON
all year

Storage:
Store opened cans of straw mushrooms in the refrigerator for up to a few days in water (not in the water from the can).

Nutrition:
Straw mushrooms are a good source of protein, and also contain B vitamins, zinc, folate, magnesium and potassium.

Straw mushrooms are oval or egg-like mushrooms, in the same way as the young horse mushrooms, and are cultivated to just reach the opening stage to keep their pleasing shape. Grown mostly on composted rice paddy straw, hence the nickname paddy straw mushrooms, they are produced mainly in Hong Kong, Thailand, Taiwan and Indonesia. Soft and squidgy, these mushrooms are very delicate and are brined and canned upon harvesting.

They are a great addition to any soup, bringing an unusual texture and a satisfying pop when you bite into them. We couldn't leave them out of our Chinese broth on page 250, but these mushrooms would go well in any coconut or spicy sauce or soup.

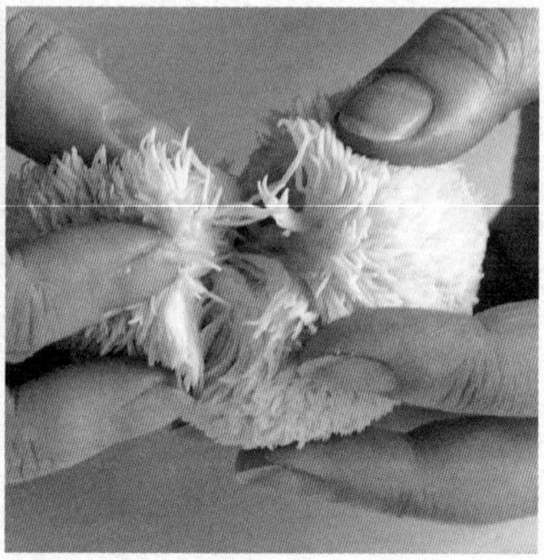

Pom pom THE CHEERLEADER

OTHER NAMES
Old man's beard, lion's mane

LATIN NAME
Hericium erinaceus

USUALLY FOUND IN
Asia, the UK, Europe

SEASON
Summer to autumn, but available all year

Storage:
Store in open containers in the refrigerator for up to two weeks.

Nutrition:
Used extensively in Chinese medicine and believed to do many good things, pom poms are good for digestion, have shown to stimulate new or brain cell growth, and help lower cholesterol. They also contain anti-bacterial, anti-inflammatory and anti-tumour properties.

The pom pom is basically a ball of elongated mushroom spines and a delight to cook with. It's exciting visually, and tastes and has the texture of seafood when cooked. Produced on logs and in substrate plastic-covered blocks, the pom pom shares similarities with the shiitake when it comes to commercial cultivation and grows out of the block once the plastic is pierced. They grow in mounds from a central group of stems and can be broken away into clumps quite easily. Grown in sterile conditions, pom poms are very clean mushrooms and just need to be rinsed gently. The pom pom is a farmed fungus and although found in the wild, mainly growing on beech trees, it is extremely rare and is in fact one of four protected fungi covered by the Wildlife and Countryside Act and so against the law to pick it.

The pom pom name makes the most sense, as it looks exactly like that. The cultivated version is a brilliant white colour and has a firm yet spongy texture, and looks fantastical in any meal. We enjoyed using them in our Portuguese mushroom risotto (see page 130) and our preserved jars of mushrooms in oil on page 142.

Black THE CUPBOARD STANDBY

OTHER NAMES
Cloud ear fungus, wood ear fungus

LATIN NAME
Auricularia polytricha

USUALLY FOUND IN
Asia

SEASON
All year

Storage:
Store in an airtight container out of direct sunlight.

Nutrition:
High in protein and low in calories, these mushrooms are key in Chinese medicine and contain vitamin K, are rich in iron and are said to counteract high cholesterol.

The black mushroom is a jelly fungus that is usually sold dried. Rubbery, brown-black and ear-shaped, this Asian mushroom grows from tree bark and is now grown in cylinders of sterilized sawdust.

The large mushroom is great rehydrated and chopped in soups and salads. Crunchy and slippery, it has a similar consistency to some seaweeds and is used in many Japanese salads. We have used it in a ramen, fish and mushroom pie and in Chinese broth (recipes on pages 206, 198 and 250). It takes 15 minutes to rehydrate this mushroom in boiling water, see below, then you can cut away and discard the hard piece usually to the side, where the mushroom grew from, and use whole or sliced.

RECIPES

MUSHROOMS IN THE KITCHEN

Although such a unique food, mushrooms blend happily into a wide range of dishes and different styles of cooking. From your common button mushroom to the pretty morel or the umami-rich cep, every mushroom has the potential to be the star of the show as well as a chorus stalwart. It's a joy to take each mushroom as they appear throughout the year.

TASTE

Mushrooms are a product of their environment, not just in their growth or colour, but in the way they taste. Some mushrooms are nutty, others are fruity, and wild mushrooms have a taste of whatever forest they have hailed from. Certain mushrooms can taste like pine, and others have an oaty or cornmeal element to them. Apricots, chestnuts, walnuts and coconut are some of the flavours that have been attributed to various mushrooms, but as with most natural foods, the experience is wonderfully subjective and different people taste different things.

The recipes in this book show many traditional and new ways of treating mushrooms, but you will want to experiment with them in the kitchen yourself. Just take care to read the mushroom profiles before embarking on cooking, as some wild mushrooms shouldn't be eaten raw, and of course always make sure you buy wild mushrooms from a reputable outlet or trusted forager.

CLEANING

Each of the mushroom profiles include step-by-step guides on how to clean that particular mushroom. In the past, cooks have tended to apply a one-rule-for-all policy when it comes to mushrooms, but this can mean that you spoil a dish by washing the super-absorbent cep or brushing mud-caked trompettes (a task with no end in sight, by the way). Some mushrooms need a gentle bath, some need delicately wiping with a wet cloth, and others just need a quick dust with a dry brush. As you get to use different mushrooms, it will become apparent how to tackle them, depending on how delicate they are, whether they are gilled, gill-less or pored, and how and where they grow – and of course how dirty they are.

Cleaning a lot of mushrooms can be tiresome, but follow the guidance and take heart in the fact that the advice gives the best and quickest way, and that the end result is more than worth it.

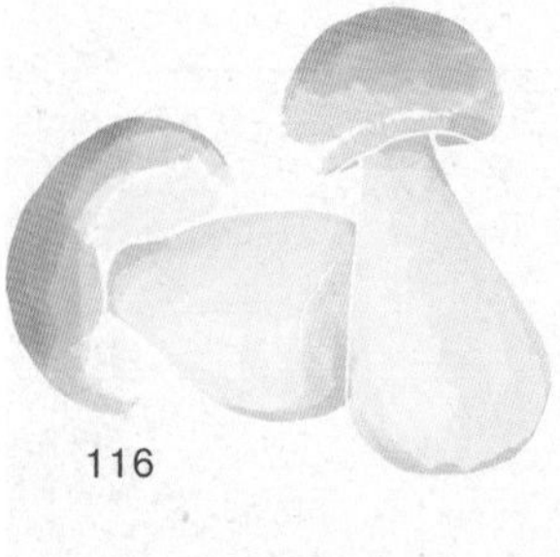

COOKING

There are many opinions out there about how to cook mushrooms in general and the different types of mushrooms. With the profiles and recipes to guide you, this book aims to take you on your own mushroom discovery, and decide what works for you. But here are a few pointers I have picked up along the way, which may help.

RAW: There is some debate about whether mushrooms are safe to eat raw, and a few wild mushrooms are known to cause stomach upsets; it is important to be very careful. However some mushrooms are considered safe to eat raw, and perhaps a shame to miss out on. When young and raw, the bright orange and yellow, egg-like caesar mushrooms have the texture of edible velvet that melts in your mouth, the taste of chestnuts and the aroma of apricot. These mushrooms are highly coveted and therefore quite expensive, and for that reason we only produced one recipe for this book, but they are also good sprinkled raw into a finished pasta dish or grilled with olive oil. Good-quality raw ceps are also great finely sliced, which brings out their almost indescribable meat-like flavour, and cultivated button mushrooms have a distinct coconut flavour when raw, which is even stronger if the mushrooms are really fresh. And of course, the superstar of the wild mushroom world, the truffle, is usually grated and finely shaved raw onto food to give the optimum flavour. A classic grated raw mushroom salad dressed with white truffle oil is pretty hard to beat, if the mushrooms are as fresh as possible (see page 180).

MAKE IT SIMPLE: Throughout the world, mushrooms are traditionally cooked and enjoyed in many forms – breaded and deep fried, sautéed in butter, added to risotto and pasta, made a soup out of, or stuffed – but I have found that it is best to go back to basics and cook them simply to give yourself a chance to get to know the different mushroom tastes. If allowed to, a mushroom's taste intensifies as it cooks, and the best way to find out what the different mushrooms are about is to simply grill them with a little olive oil and then add seasoning – sea salt should bring out the flavours. With some warm fresh bread and maybe some capers or lemon juice, this is already a great meal (go to page 216 for the recipe), but of course there are many exciting discoveries to be made as you take the mushroom further in the kitchen.

VEGETARIAN STEAK: A great meat substitute, the larger and more bulkier mushrooms like ceps, flat or portobello, eryngii, larger shiitake and pied de mouton can be cooked just like meat, but for less time, with roasting, braising, pan frying and poaching all working well.

PERFECT PAIRINGS: Good food matches do change with the season and the type of mushroom. Asian types of mushrooms generally lend themselves well to stir-fries and tempura batter, and wild mushrooms will be at home in a modern-European garlic and cream sauce, but if we can forget our preconceptions there are many other tempting taste combinations out there.

Shiitake mushrooms, for one instance, seem to go with anything. Their rich woody taste complements all kinds of vegetables, both strong-tasting and delicate. You can try pairing them with kale, tomatoes, aubergine, cabbage and asparagus. They also help make a great gravy and really add to a roast beef dish, along with some beef tomatoes, garlic and fresh parsley.

I would put button and closed-cup mushrooms in anything and everything, whatever the season and whether it's Asian or European style, sautéed or roasted, poached or grilled. There's a good reason why they are the most cultivated and bought mushroom worldwide. Oyster mushrooms are great with fish – poached, fried or roasted – their soft-yet-firm texture and delicate flavour complements most fish and seafood, and they seem to belong together.

Seasonally, in spring wild mushrooms such as morels and St George's can be found paired with asparagus and wild garlic, and summer mushrooms such as girolles and caesars can be found with lighter ingredients like basil, lemon and samphire. When we get to autumn – the time for wild mushrooms – flavours get deeper, with ceps and chanterelles getting along brilliantly with game, blackberries and apples. Wintertime sees trompettes as a main ingredient in pastas with thyme and orange to bring out the earthy tones, and pied de mouton being paired with black pudding in stews.

All mushrooms are good with garlic. That's pretty much a fact. But, not all agree with butter... That's another issue that can be left up to taste.

DRIED: Mushrooms change character and flavour completely when they have been dried and should be treated quite differently in the kitchen. A chef once said to me that dried mushrooms add flavour and fresh mushrooms carry flavour, and although I don't quite think that's true for all fresh mushrooms (you can't get away from the taste of a lobster mushroom, pied de mouton or mousseron mushroom, to name a few), it's a pretty apt description of dried.

You can get quite a few different types of dried mushrooms commercially (and of course have a go at drying them yourself). The main dried types are cep, which are more commonly known as porcini when dried, morel, whole shiitake, and trompette – they also come in mixed bags. In general, mushrooms should be rehydrated in boiling water (enough to cover them) for 15 minutes so they are soft and malleable. They are really tasty added to a soufflé or omelette or cooked as part of a sauce or in a soup. When cooking with them, where you would possibly add a fresh mushroom towards the end of the cooking time to preserve its texture and taste, you add dried at the beginning so they will be completely soft and edible, as well as flavouring the entire meal. Don't throw away the water after you drain the mushrooms, as it makes a great stock to use in other dishes or even the same dish, which you'll see in a lot of the recipes in this book.

SPRING

These recipes make the most of the important springtime mushrooms, St George's, morels and mousserons, whilst also using some year-round cultivated mushrooms that suit the new season nicely.

Rabbit is particularly plentiful just as the morels come out, so this is the perfect time to make the most of both of these natural spring offerings. Rabbit meat can be on the dry side, but 'pulling it' with chocolate and paprika makes for a succulent, sticky treat combined with the earthy, savoury morel mushrooms. Making your own pasta can be a joy and you don't have to use a pasta machine for this ravioli recipe – just a lot of elbow grease! Whether you use a machine or not, you do have to act quickly before the pasta dries out, so no dilly dallying. If you love cooking, this is the perfect way to spend a crisp spring day.

Pulled rabbit and morel ravioli

Serves 4–6
Ready in 6 hours
(including 5 hours slow-cooking and chilling time)

PULLED RABBIT

- 30ml/2 tbsp sweet paprika
- 20g/¾oz dark (bittersweet) chocolate, grated
- 50g/2oz soft brown sugar
- 1 garlic clove, crushed
- 30ml/2 tbsp white wine vinegar
- 60ml/4 tbsp olive oil
- 300ml/½ pint/1¼ cups sweet cider
- 1 prepared rabbit (skinned and gutted)
- 100g/3¾oz morels, chopped
- Zest and juice of 1 lemon
- 100g/3¾oz wild garlic, ripped into shreds

RAVIOLI

- 400g/14oz/3½ cups plain (all-purpose) flour, sifted, plus extra for dusting
- 3 large eggs, beaten
- 15g/1 tbsp crushed pink peppercorns
- Sea salt and ground black peppercorns

1 Preheat the oven to 150°C/300°F/Gas 2. Combine the paprika, chocolate, sugar, garlic, vinegar and 30ml/2 tbsp of the olive oil in a large bowl, then coat the rabbit with the mixture. Fill a roasting pan with the cider, then place the coated rabbit in it. Cover with foil and cook for 3 hours, basting every hour. Remove the foil and turn the oven to 140°C/275°F/Gas 1, then cook for a further 2 hours. Place the cooked rabbit on a plate, shred the meat with two forks and remove the bones. Transfer the meat to a large bowl.

2 In a pan, add 15ml/1 tbsp of the oil and fry the morel mushrooms for 2–3 minutes, until soft, then add half the lemon juice and half the wild garlic. Stir and then transfer to the bowl of rabbit meat. Mix thoroughly.

> *Recipe continues overleaf*

PER SERVING: ENERGY 445KCAL/1881KJ | PROTEIN 29.5GG | CARBOHYDRATE 65.2G, OF WHICH SUGARS 12.6G | FAT 8.8G, OF WHICH SATURATES 3.2G | CHOLESTEROL 192MG | CALCIUM 159MG | FIBRE 3.1G | SODIUM 92MG.

3 Place the flour in a large bowl and make a well in the middle with your fist and pour the eggs into it. Using a fork, whisk the flour into the egg from the outside in. When the mixture begins to come together, shape it into a ball with your hands, then knead for 10 minutes. Divide the dough into four, then wrap individually with clear film or plastic wrap and chill for 5 minutes.

4 On a floured surface, roll out one of the balls into a rectangle (20 x 30cm/8 x 12in), so it is extremely thin, and then with a sharp knife or ravioli wheel, cut into four equal strips. Dot five teaspoons of the rabbit and morel mixture on two of the strips as filling for the ravioli.

5 Brush cold water on to the pasta around the filling, then place the other strips of the pasta exactly on top and press down with your first two fingertips to seal around the edges and in between the filling. Cut in between the filling to make 5 ravioli. Chill them, divided by clear film or plastic wrap.

6 Repeat the process with the other 3 pasta balls, whilst the others chill, to make 20 in total. In a large pan, cook the ravioli in boiling water for 5–6 minutes, drain and refresh. In a frying pan, heat the remaining 15ml/1 tbsp oil, then add the wild garlic and lemon zest and remaining juice.

7 Stir-fry for 1 minute. Coat the pasta with the olive oil mixture and season with salt and crushed peppercorns, then divide between warmed plates and serve immediately.

Warming, filling and rich, focaccia is a great platform for three bounties of spring: the morel mushroom, wild garlic and asparagus. Earthy, naturally sweet and aromatically allium-like, these flavours combine with the comfortingly soft, moist bread, which you'll enjoy baking (and smelling) as much as eating.

Morel, wild garlic and asparagus focaccia

Makes 1 large loaf
Ready in 1 hour, plus resting

- 500g/1¼lb strong wholemeal (whole-wheat) flour
- 500g/1¼lb strong white flour, plus extra for dusting
- 10g/2 tsp pink peppercorns, crushed, plus extra to garnish
- 7g/2½ tsp fast-action yeast
- 500ml/17fl oz/generous 2 cups warm water
- 100ml/3.5fl oz/½ cup extra virgin rapeseed oil, plus extra for greasing and drizzling
- 100g/3¾oz wild garlic, ripped into shreds
- 200g/7oz asparagus, sliced in half vertically and roughly chopped
- 200g/7oz morels or any other spring or cultivated mushrooms, sliced lengthways
- Zest of 1 lemon
- Sea salt

1 In a large bowl, combine the two flours, 1 tsp of the pink peppercorns and a pinch of salt. Make a well in the middle of the flour with your fist and sprinkle the yeast into it. Mix together warm water and 85ml/3fl oz/¾ cup of the oil in a jug or pitcher and pour into the well. Stir in a figure-of-eight motion, until a dough forms.

2 Knead the dough by pushing the dough over itself in a folding motion, continuously, in the bowl for 10 minutes, adding further flour if needed. On a floured surface, knead in the wild garlic, then asparagus and morels, retaining a few pieces of both for decoration. Transfer the dough to a clean bowl, cover with oiled clear film or plastic wrap and a clean dish towel, and place in a warm place to prove for 30 minutes.

3 Preheat the oven to 220°C/425°F/Gas 7 and grease an A4-size rectangular flat baking sheet. Knock back the dough, by pushing the air out of it with your fist. On a surface lightly dusted with flour, knead half the lemon zest into the dough for 2 minutes, then stretch the dough out to fit the prepared baking sheet.

4 Push about 12 spaced-out dents into the bread with your thumb and top with the remaining pink peppercorns, asparagus and morels, then drizzle with the remaining 15ml/1 tbsp oil. Cover with the dish towel and leave to prove again for 20 minutes. After proving, bake for 20–25 minutes, until risen and golden. Brush with more oil and serve, garnished with the remaining lemon zest, pink peppercorns and salt.

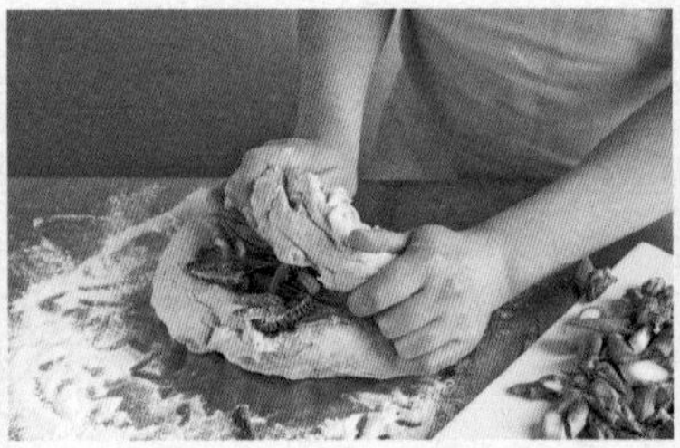

PER SERVING: ENERGY 329KCAL/1391KJ | PROTEIN 10.3G | CARBOHYDRATE 59.5G, OF WHICH SUGARS 2.0G | FAT 7G, OF WHICH SATURATES 1.0G | CHOLESTEROL 0MG | CALCIUM 94MG | FIBRE 7.5G | SODIUM 15MG.

A Portuguese risotto is a cross between a paella and a risotto, with sharp olives and preserved lemons giving the creaminess of the rice a tart contrast. Portugal has a long history of using wild mushrooms in cooking, as well as commercial foraging. You can use any kind of mushroom in this risotto – add the more delicate ones towards the end and the sturdier mushrooms at the beginning. We have added some cultivated pom pom and horse mushrooms into the mix too, to give a bit more texture.

Portuguese wild mushroom risotto

Serves 4
Ready in 45 minutes

- 40g/1½oz dried ceps
- 2 saffron threads
- 15ml/1 tbsp olive oil
- 15g/1 tbsp butter
- 4 garlic cloves, whole
- 1 onion, chopped
- 2.5g/½ tsp sugar
- 200g/7oz St George's mushrooms, chopped
- 100g/3¾oz horse or button (white) mushrooms
- 400g/14oz risotto rice
- 125ml/4fl oz/½ cup white wine
- 1 preserved lemon, chopped, plus extra to serve
- 100g/3¾oz pom poms, chopped
- 200g/7oz morels, chopped
- 400g/14oz canned tomatoes, chopped
- 100g/3¾oz green olives, pitted
- 7g/2½ tsp chopped fresh flat leaf parsley
- Sea salt and ground black pepper

1 Place the dried ceps in a jug or pitcher and fill with 1 litre/1¾ pints/4 cups of boiling water, then add the saffron. Stand for 10 minutes.

2 Meanwhile, in a large pan, heat the olive oil and butter, then add the whole garlic cloves and chopped onion, and then sprinkle with the sugar. Sauté for 5 minutes, until the onions are soft. Stir in the St George's mushrooms and horse or button mushrooms and cook for 1 minute. Season with a pinch of salt, then add the rice, stirring to coat with the mixture. Stir in the wine and lemon, then bring to a high simmer to reduce the liquid. Add a ladle of the cep and saffron water, and reduce it down, stirring as you go.

3 Remove the rehydrated dried ceps from the saffron water, chop and add to the pan. Continue to add the saffron water, a ladle at a time, reducing it each time, whilst constantly stirring. This should take around 20 minutes.

4 Stir in the pom pom mushrooms, morel mushrooms and the canned tomatoes and reduce down again, stirring constantly for 2 minutes. Mix in the olives and parsley, then season with salt and pepper, and serve.

PER SERVING: ENERGY 494KCAL/2064KJ | PROTEIN 11.4G | CARBOHYDRATE 83.7G, OF WHICH SUGARS 3.4G | FAT 10G, OF WHICH SATURATES 2.9G | CHOLESTEROL 8MG | CALCIUM 62MG | FIBRE 4.2G | SODIUM 634MG.

A great centrepiece for a special occasion, this pâté is full of strong earthy flavours, from the rich duck livers seared in butter to the hearty morels and smooth whiskey. If you get your hands on some morels, this is a good way to show off their peculiar tree-like shape, giving your dinner party or supper a super-seasonal talking point. But of course, any wild mushrooms would go well in this pâté, all adding something different to the end dish. The pâté takes three hours to set or preferably it should be chilled overnight, so be sure to plan ahead.

Duck and morel pâté

Serves 6–8 as an appetizer
Ready in 20 minutes, plus cooling and overnight chilling

- 25g/1oz/2 tbsp butter, plus extra for greasing
- 5ml/1 tsp olive oil
- 500g/1¼lb duck livers, cutting away any sinew
- 1 garlic clove, crushed
- 200g/7oz morels, halved horizontally
- 50ml/2fl oz/¼ cup non-peat vanilla-like whiskey
- 25ml/1½ tbsp double (heavy) cream
- Zest and juice of 1 orange
- 7g/2½ tsp chopped fresh flat leaf parsley
- Ground black pepper

1 In a large frying pan, heat the butter with the oil and fry the duck livers for about 2 minutes, until sealed all over. Remove with a slotted spoon and then add the garlic and morels. Fry, stirring, for 2 minutes, then season with pepper. Remove the morels with a slotted spoon and set aside. Return the livers to the pan and cook for another minute, before adding the whiskey. Simmer for 2 minutes, until the whiskey is reduced and the flavours are sucked up by the livers. The livers should be cooked through completely. Allow to cool for 5 minutes.

2 In a large food processor or using a hand blender, blend the liver mixture with the cream, orange zest and juice, parsley and half of the morels, then mix in the remaining sliced morels without blending, saving a few for decoration.

3 Grease and then line a pâté dish or 900g/2lb loaf tin or pan with clear film or plastic wrap, sprinkle pepper into it and scatter with the reserved morel slices. Fill with the liver mixture, smoothing out the top with a spatula. Chill for at least 3 hours or overnight until set. To serve, turn out on to a serving board or plate, using the film to manoeuvre, and accompany with toast or crusty bread.

PER SERVING: ENERGY 119KCAL/495KJ | PROTEIN 11.6G | CARBOHYDRATE 0.7G, OF WHICH SUGARS 0.7G | FAT 6.2G, OF WHICH SATURATES 3.2G | CHOLESTEROL 248MG | CALCIUM 9MG | FIBRE 0.4G | SODIUM 69MG.

One of the prettiest mushrooms and a signal that spring is well underway with summer fast behind, mousserons jazz up an everyday pastry tart and complement their nuttier and sturdier cultivated cousins, the chestnut, with a delicate texture and strong taste. Both mushrooms take hardly any time at all to bake and the tiny mousserons turn almost crispy.

Chestnut mushroom and mousseron tart

Serves 4
Ready in 55 mins, plus chilling

225g/8oz/2 cups strong flour, sifted, plus extra for dusting
110g/4oz chilled butter, cubed, plus extra for greasing
110g/4oz chilled lard, cubed
125ml/4fl oz/generous ½ cup iced water
250g/8fl oz/1 cup ricotta cheese
30g/2 tbsp chopped fresh thyme, plus extra to garnish
30g/2 tbsp freshly grated nutmeg
Zest and juice of 1 lemon
150g/5oz chestnut mushrooms, sliced
100g/3¾oz mousserons
15ml/1 tbsp olive oil
1 egg, beaten
Salt and ground black pepper

Tip: This pastry is a fresh and zingy rough-puff, but you can make the tart more quickly by buying ready-made puff pastry and skipping to step 3 of the recipe.

1 In a large bowl, place the flour with a pinch of salt, then add the butter and lard. Stir, then make a well with your fist in the centre. Pour the water in and then stir together until it comes together in a ball.

2 Lightly dust a surface and rolling pin with flour, then shape the dough with your hands into a rectangle on the surface. Roll out into a longer rectangle, then fold one third over to the middle to cover another third and then fold the remaining side over too, dusting more flour over the pastry if it becomes sticky. Turn around, so the folds face you, and repeat the process. Do this three more times, then wrap in clear film or plastic wrap and chill for 2 hours.

3 Let the pastry come up to room temperature, then roll into a 16 x 12cm/6¼ x 4½in rectangle and cut into 8 equal rectangles. With a sharp knife, cut out inner rectangles from 4 of the shapes and place on top of the other 4 to create finger-width borders, brushing with beaten egg to secure in place. Place on a greased baking sheet and chill for 15 minutes.

4 Preheat the oven to 210°C/410°F/Gas 7. In a bowl, mix together the ricotta, thyme, nutmeg and lemon zest and juice, then season. Fill the pastry shapes with the ricotta mixture and top with the mushrooms, layering them over each other if necessary. Drizzle with the olive oil. Bake for 15 minutes, then turn the oven down to 190°C/375°F/Gas 5 for a further 15 minutes. Garnish with thyme and serve immediately.

PER SERVING: ENERGY 818KCAL/3395KJ | PROTEIN 14.3G | CARBOHYDRATE 46.3G, OF WHICH SUGARS 1.1G | FAT 65.2G, OF WHICH SATURATES 33.1G | CHOLESTEROL 162MG | CALCIUM 157MG | FIBRE 3.3G | SODIUM 406MG.

All the joy of bread with none of the hassle, flatbreads are an excellent quick fix when you need something fancy in a hurry. They are also great for an open sandwich or light lunch. Our springtime friends the morels are a perfect shape for flatbreads, producing a pleasing flower shape if sliced horizontally. The tiny cultivated shimeji add a sweet-flavoured touch to the earthy morel, and a simple homemade garlic oil – just crush the garlic and add it to the oil – makes for a tasty treat. And, no proving needed!

Morel and shimeji flatbreads

Makes 6
Ready in 20 minutes

- 400g/14oz/3½ cups plain (all-purpose) flour, plus extra for dusting
- 15g/1 tbsp crushed pink peppercorns
- 150ml/¼ pint/⅔ cup water
- 75ml/5 tbsp extra virgin olive oil
- 100g/3¾oz morels, sliced
- 20g/¾oz brown shimeji, halved
- 10ml/2 tsp fennel seeds
- Sea salt
- Garlic oil and balsamic vinegar, to serve

1 Place the flour, pinch of sea salt and pink peppercorns, water and oil in a large bowl and mix together thoroughly with a spatula. Dust your hands with flour, then knead the dough, by folding it on to itself again and again, for 5 minutes. Gently knead in the morels, shimeji and fennel seeds.

2 Dust a clean surface with flour, then divide the dough into six pieces or a couple of large ones, depending on whether you'd like to make individual or large flatbreads. Don't forget to conside the size of your griddle or frying pan – the flatbreads will have to fit on it to cook completely. Dust with flour and roll each out to about 5mm/¼in thick, whichever size you choose.

3 Preheat a griddle or frying pan to hot, then add one flatbread, flipping after 1–2 minutes when one side has browned slightly and then cooking the other side for 1 minute, or until cooked.

4 Transfer to a warmed plate and continue with the remaining flatbreads. Serve warm with the garlic oil and balsamic vinegar, and extra sea salt.

PER FLATBREAD: 312KCAL/1317KJ | PROTEIN 6.9G | CARBOHYDRATE 51.9G, OF WHICH SUGARS 1G | FAT 10.4G, OF WHICH SATURATES 1.5G | CHOLESTEROL 0MG | CALCIUM 115MG | FIBRE 3.1G | SODIUM 5MG.

A triumphal seasonal fusion, St George's, morels and wild boar work together like the Three Musketeers, combining to give a powerful punch of flavour, aroma and texture. Dried morels rehydrated in hot water and drained will work just as well for this recipe if you can't find fresh. Making your own sausages isn't that scary, especially when you have mastered the piping action. You can usually order sausage skins from a butcher and any leftover skins can be frozen or will keep in the refrigerator for up to three months.

Wild mushroom and boar sausages

Makes 10–12 sausages
Ready in 30 minutes

- 2 garlic cloves, chopped
- 400g/14oz wild boar shoulder, finely chopped
- 200g/7oz St George's mushrooms
- 100g/3¾oz morels
- 3 portobello or field mushrooms
- 15g/1 tbsp smoked paprika
- 7g/1½ tsp finely chopped fresh sage
- 50ml/2fl oz/¼ cup red wine
- 1 pack of sausage skins
- Sea salt and ground white pepper
- Green salad and wholegrain mustard, to serve

1 In a food processor, roughly blend the garlic, wild boar, St George's, morels, portobello mushrooms, paprika, sage and wine, and season with salt and pepper.

2 Fill the mixture into a piping bag and roll the sausage skins up as you would a sock. Slowly but forcefully pipe the mixture into the sausage skins, holding the rolled sausage skins securely around the piping nozzle, to make sausages about the length of your finger, twisting the skins in between each one. Chill until you are ready to cook them (or for no longer than 2 days).

3 When ready, snip them with scissors into separate sausages, where you twisted them to separate, and cook them on a preheated griddle pan, grill or broiler for 5–7 minutes, turning a couple of times, until cooked through and browned.

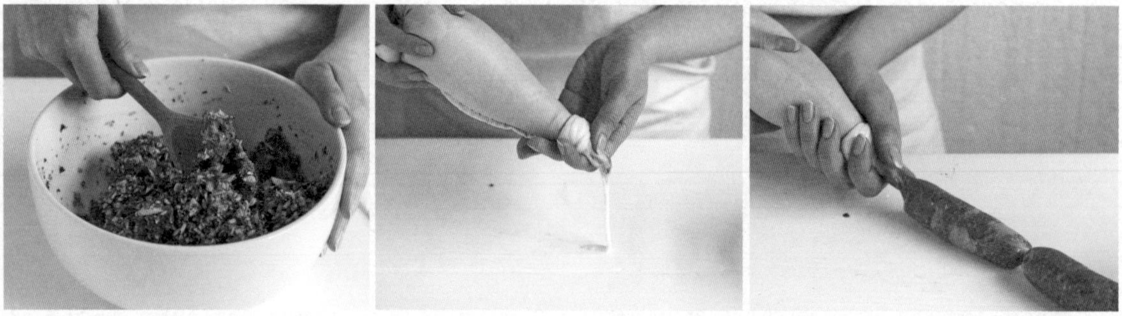

PER SAUSAGE: ENERGY 118KCAL/493KJ | PROTEIN 10G | CARBOHYDRATE 0.6G, OF WHICH SUGARS 0.1G | FAT 8.2G, OF WHICH SATURATES 3.2G | CHOLESTEROL 32MG | CALCIUM 8MG | FIBRE 0.6G | SODIUM 29MG.

The milk in these fluffy and soft bread rolls is infused with fresh ceps, letting all the sugars and distinct forest flavours take over the dough. Inspired by innovative vegetarian London restaurant Vanilla Black, who gave Liz the idea of flavouring milk with ceps, the recipe brings out the caramel tones of the ceps with a touch of vanilla bean paste and refreshes them anew. Dried cep mushrooms (known as porcini) can be used instead of fresh, but the taste will be different and more intense. Whichever form of cep you use, be sure to allow the milk to cool down to room temperature before adding it to the dough, as if it is any hotter it could kill the yeast and result in tough bread.

Plaited milk cep rolls

Makes 8
Ready in 1 hour 20 minutes

50g/2oz ceps, finely sliced
50g/2oz/4 tbsp butter
100ml/3½fl oz/scant ½ cup milk
50ml/2fl oz/¼ cup single (light) cream
5g/1 tsp vanilla bean paste
5g/1 tsp caster (superfine) sugar
250g/9oz/2¼ cups strong white flour, sifted, plus extra for dusting
7g/2½ tsp active dried yeast
2.5ml/½ tsp salt
2 eggs, beaten

1 Place the ceps, butter, milk, cream and vanilla in a pan and simmer on a low heat, without boiling, for 5 minutes. Drain the liquid into a jug or pitcher, reserving the mushrooms. Allow the liquid to stand until room temperature, then mix in the sugar.

2 Place the flour in a large bowl and make a well with your fist in the middle. Add the yeast and salt, and then 1 beaten egg. Pour in the milk mixture, mixing in a figure-of-eight with a spatula until the dough comes together. Knead in the bowl for 10 minutes, then cover with oiled clear film or plastic wrap and a damp clean dish towel making sure it is airtight. Stand in a warm place to prove for 1 hour or until doubled in size.

3 Knock back the dough with your fist to remove the air, then knead in the reserved mushrooms. Turn on to a surface lightly dusted with flour and cut into eight equal pieces. Roll each piece into a sausage shape, then from the top, cut three equal strands. Plait the bread together to make a roll shape and then seal the ends by squeezing together. Repeat for each plait. Place on a baking sheet lined with baking parchment and cover with oiled clear film and a damp cloth. Prove for 30 minutes in a warm place. Preheat the oven to 200°C/400°F/Gas 6.

4 Brush with the remaining beaten egg, then bake for 20 minutes until slightly golden. Serve with butter.

PER ROLL: ENERGY 194KCAL/816KJ | PROTEIN 5.5G | CARBOHYDRATE 25.8G, OF WHICH SUGARS 1.9G | FAT 8.4G, OF WHICH SATURATES 4.6G | CHOLESTEROL 66MG | CALCIUM 72MG | FIBRE 1.4G | SODIUM 66MG.

When springtime finally hits after an always-too-long winter, it's the first flush of St George's mushroom that really signals the start of warmer days and more plentiful surroundings. And when it comes to mushrooms, it can feel like a long wait, again, for the abundance of autumn, so this is a great way to preserve a taste of spring. And, of course, you can do this all over again when you get to the mighty cep in autumn. The mushrooms will last three months and can include any types of mushrooms, as well as different ingredients to flavour. This accompaniment is nice with meats or in sauces, or simply on their own.

Mushrooms in oil

Makes 2 x 500g/1¼lb jars
Ready in 20 minutes, plus 13 hours standing time

- 1kg/2¼lb mousserons, enoki, shimeji, pom poms, St George's, horse and button (white) mushrooms, roughly chopped
- Sea salt
- 700ml/1⅓ pint/scant 3 cups white vinegar
- 1 head of garlic, broken into cloves
- 4 bay leaves
- 500ml/17fl oz/generous 2 cups rapeseed oil
- Pink peppercorns

1 Place all the mushrooms on a large plate or a couple of plates and cover liberally with salt. Stand for 1 hour. Brush off and discard any salt and pat the mushrooms dry with kitchen paper.

2 Pour the vinegar into a pan, then bring to the boil. Add the mushrooms, garlic, bay leaves and pink peppercorns and simmer for 10 minutes, then dry on kitchen paper. Leave to dry on trays for 12 hours. Pack into sterilized jars and fill up with oil. Chill for a week, then eat. If kept in the refrigerator, they will last for 3 months.

PER JAR: ENERGY 1414KCAL/5819KJ | PROTEIN 9G | CARBOHYDRATE 2G, OF WHICH SUGARS 1G | FAT 152.4G, OF WHICH SATURATES 10.4G | CHOLESTEROL 0MG | CALCIUM 30MG | FIBRE 7.4G | SODIUM 25MG.

SUMMER

SUMMER

A wild mushroom momentum builds through summertime, leading up to the all-abundant autumn. It's also a time to experiment with all the cultivated mushrooms that suit lighter seasonal dishes.

Proving mushroom soups aren't just for autumn, this quick-to-make creamy and fragrant dish welcomes the widely cultivated shiitake mushroom into a traditional British recipe. The shiitake has the most intense umami flavour of all the mushrooms and brings a lot of elements that meat would. With soft, coconut-like button mushrooms and fleshy portobello mushrooms supporting, this is a great filling soup for a cool summer's day, reminding you that the thrill of mushroom-abundant autumn is on its way. Smoked salt is ace and really brings out the favour of the mushrooms, but sea salt will also do the job.

Creamy mixed mushroom and tarragon soup

Serves 4–6
Ready in 30 minutes

- 5g/1 tsp butter
- 5ml/1 tsp olive oil
- 2 garlic cloves, crushed
- 200g/7oz shiitake, sliced
- 200g/7oz button (white) mushrooms, sliced
- 4 portobello mushrooms, sliced
- 10g/3 tbsp tarragon, chopped, plus extra for garnish
- 5g/1 tsp palm sugar or caster (superfine) sugar
- 1 litre/1¾ pints/4 cups vegetable stock
- 2 bay leaves
- 100ml/3½fl oz/scant ½ cup crème fraîche
- Juice of ½ lemon
- 5g/1 tsp ground pink peppercorns
- Smoked salt and ground black pepper
- Crusty bread, to serve

1 In a large pan, heat the butter and oil, then add the garlic. Sauté for 1 minute, then add all the mushrooms and the tarragon, sautéing for 4–5 minutes, until golden. Add the palm sugar, stock and bay leaves, and then bring to the boil, simmering for 20 minutes.

2 Stir in the crème fraîche, lemon juice and pink peppercorns. Season with smoked salt and black pepper, garnish with extra tarragon and serve with crusty bread.

PER SERVING: ENERGY 90KCAL/373KJ | PROTEIN 2.2G | CARBOHYDRATE 1.6G, OF WHICH SUGARS 1.3G | FAT 8.4G, OF WHICH SATURATES 5.1G | CHOLESTEROL 21MG | CALCIUM 19MG | FIBRE 1.5G | SODIUM 14MG.

There's nothing like the hot melt-in-your-mouth taste sensation of this South American-inspired dish. Combining very pretty pink, grey and yellow oyster mushrooms with traditional salted and citrus-cured fish, soy sauce and sesame oil, onion and chilli, it is also a nod to the fashionable fusion of Peruvian and Japanese cuisine, called 'Nikkei', perfect for anyone who loves strong flavours and eclectic textures. The best ceviche is always served chilled, which is why this recipe includes a good deal of chilling at various stages – you'll appreciate the difference! It is excellent served with tortilla chips.

Mushroom ceviche

Serves 2
Ready in 10 minutes, plus chilling

- 300g/11oz sea bass fillet, sliced very thinly against the grain
- 300g/11oz mixed-colour oyster mushrooms, roughly ripped apart
- Zest and juice of 3 limes
- 1 red onion, finely chopped
- 1 red chilli, chopped
- 7g/2½ tsp micro coriander cress, or chopped fresh coriander (cilantro)
- 15ml/1 tbsp toasted sesame oil
- 5ml/1 tsp soy sauce
- 5g/1 tsp pink peppercorns
- Sea salt

1 In a large bowl, place the fish slices and the mushrooms and sprinkle with a good pinch of sea salt. Cover with clear film or plastic wrap, then chill for 5 minutes. Drain, and then add the lime juice and zest to the bowl and stir thoroughly. Re-cover and chill for a further 5 minutes.

2 Mix in the red onion, chilli and coriander, then chill, covered, for a further 5 minutes. On two plates, arrange the mushrooms and fish, removing them from the mixture with a fork or slotted spoon, and dress with the sesame oil and soy sauce.

3 Garnish with the pink peppercorns, crushing the peppercorns between your finger and thumb, then sprinkling. Serve immediately.

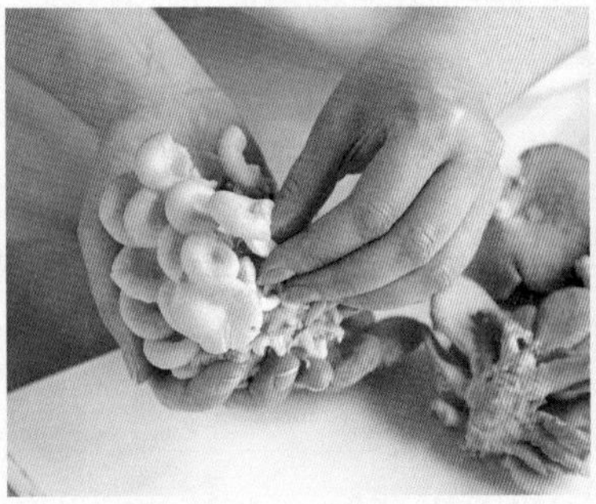
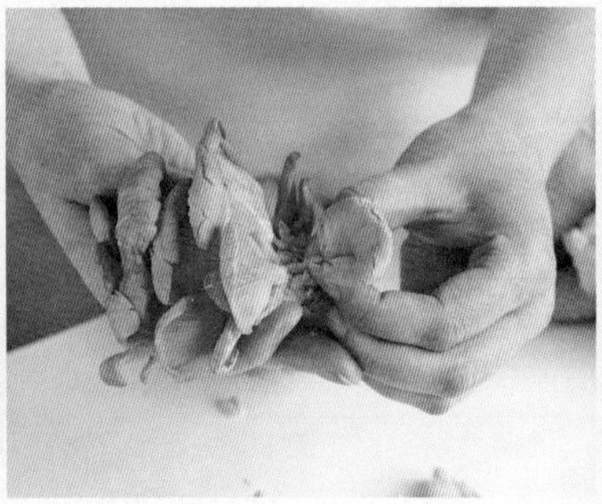

PER SERVING: ENERGY 234KCAL/978KJ | PROTEIN 32.2G | CARBOHYDRATE 3.7G, OF WHICH SUGARS 2.7G | FAT 10.1G, OF WHICH SATURATES 1.6G | CHOLESTEROL 120MG | CALCIUM 215MG | FIBRE 2.8G | SODIUM 291MG.

Taking oyster mushrooms back to their home territory, these Asian-influence canapés combine fresh-tasting seared salmon and tuna with soft and smoky oyster mushrooms, zingy pickled ginger, and raw mustardy shiso leaves, to really wake up your tastebuds. Once you have all of your components in front of you, the canapés are quick and easy to assemble – making them ideal for a dinner party where you'd rather be enjoying the food with your friends than cooking it. Also, lightly griddled oyster mushrooms make a great base for the canapés.

Oyster mushroom canapés

Makes 15
Ready in 15 minutes

- 60ml/4 tbsp soy sauce
- 50g/2oz/4 tbsp sugar
- 200g/7oz oyster mushrooms, pulled apart into bitesize pieces
- Juice of ½ lemon
- 200g/7oz tuna steak
- 200g/7oz salmon fillet
- 3g/1 tbsp fresh coriander (cilantro), finely chopped
- 15 shiso leaves
- 15g/½oz pickled ginger, shredded
- 1 nori sheet, snipped into slices

1 In a pan, combine the soy sauce with the sugar and bring to the boil. Simmer for 5 minutes, then remove from the heat. Set aside to cool and thicken.

2 Preheat a griddle pan. Place the oyster mushrooms in a dish and coat with the lemon juice. Griddle for 1 minute on each side, then set aside. In another dish, place the tuna and salmon and sprinkle over the coriander, covering completely. Griddle for 1 minute on each side and allow to rest, off the heat, for 1 minute. Slice into thin strips, against the grain of the fish.

3 On a serving plate, lay out the shiso leaves and top each with a piece of griddled mushroom, a slice of fish and a pinch of the pickled ginger and nori. Drizzle with the soy mixture (made in step 1) and serve immediately.

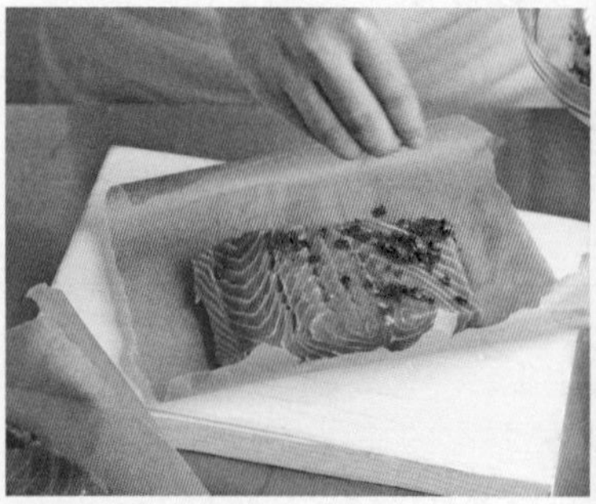

PER CANAPÉ: ENERGY 60KCAL/253KJ | PROTEIN 6.3G | CARBOHYDRATE 4.1G, OF WHICH SUGARS 4G | FAT 2.2G, OF WHICH SATURATES 0.4G | CHOLESTEROL 10MG | CALCIUM 9MG | FIBRE 0.3G | SODIUM 298MG.

Perfect for a picnic or summer buffet spread, this mushroom pork pie takes us back to farmhouse cooking basics with a sturdy hot crust pastry and a jellified meat, mushroom and wholegrain mustard filling. It's easy to achieve this if you take it step by step and make sure you have allowed enough time to complete it. The addition of nutty chestnut mushrooms, delicately flavoured woodland girolles and robust pied bleu to a traditional recipe makes for interesting textures and tastes – a forest in a pie.

Mushroom pork pie

Serves 4–6
Ready in 2 hours 20 minutes, plus overnight chilling

- 100g/3¾oz pistachio nuts, roughly crushed
- 100g/3¾oz chestnut mushrooms, halved
- 100g/3¾oz pied bleu
- 100g/3¾oz mini girolles
- 500g/1¼lb pork belly, minced (ground)
- 400g/14oz pork chops, chopped
- 200g/7oz streaky (fatty) bacon, chopped
- 15g/1 tbsp freshly grated nutmeg
- 15g/1 tbsp fresh thyme, chopped
- 200g/7oz/scant 1 cup lard
- 500g/1¼lb/scant 4½ cups plain (all-purpose) flour, plus extra for dusting
- 1 large egg yolk, beaten
- 6 x 7g gelatine leaves
- 30g/2 tbsp wholegrain mustard
- Salt and white pepper

1 Preheat the oven to 180°C/350°F/Gas 4. In a large bowl, mix together the nuts, mushrooms, pork belly, pork chops, bacon, nutmeg and thyme. Season with lots of white pepper and stir. Leave to stand.

2 In a large pan, combine 200ml/7fl oz/scant 1 cup boiling water with the lard. While the lard melts on a medium heat, sift the flour into a bowl and add a pinch of salt, then make a well in the middle. Bring the lard and water up to the boil and then as it boils, pour it into the flour and mix quickly together with a wooden spoon until a smooth, golden dough. Turn the dough out on to a clean, floured surface, then when cool enough, knead for 5 minutes, until a little firmer.

3 Put aside a third of the pastry, then roll out the remaining dough to a circle large enough to fit a 20cm/8in springform tin or pan and fit it into the tin, shaping where necessary and letting the excess overlap the sides. Fill the pie with the reserved mushroom and pork filling. Roll out the remaining third of pastry dough and place on top of the pie, pinching the edge and sides together to secure, and make a hole in the top.

4 Place the pie on a flat baking sheet and cook in the oven for 30 minutes. Turn the oven to 160°C/325°F/Gas 3 and cook for a further 1 hour 30 minutes. Remove the pie from the oven and brush the top with the egg yolk and cook for a final 20 minutes. Allow to cool completely.

5 Soak the gelatine leaves in cold water for 5 minutes. Mix 300ml/½ pint/1¼ cups water with the mustard and heat in a pan, then squeeze the water out of the gelatine leaves and add to the pan. Stir until the gelatine dissolves and allow to cool. Using a mini funnel, pour the liquid into the pie through the hole made in the top, then chill overnight or at least 4 hours to set.

PER SERVING: ENERGY 1069KCAL/4460KJ | PROTEIN 51.5G | CARBOHYDRATE 66.2G, OF WHICH SUGARS 2.2G | FAT 69.3G, OF WHICH SATURATES 24.7G | CHOLESTEROL 182MG | CALCIUM 174MG | FIBRE 5.5G | SODIUM 696MG.

This recipe was rustled up after Michael brought to the cooking studio a dryad's saddle that he'd found in the park while walking his dog Truffle that morning. Liz set to work and produced a tasty and healthy salad that showcases the beautifully full and fluffy dryad's saddle as the main player, with tiny, pretty-as-a-picture mousserons playing second fiddle. The griddled dryad's saddle and caramelized mousserons come together nicely with the bitter edible viola flowers, crunchy chickpeas, sweet wild asparagus and tangy red grapefruit. Dryad's saddle mushrooms are rarely found in shops or markets and if you can't find them just swap for portobello mushrooms.

Chickpea, dryad's saddle, mousseron and herb salad

Serves 2–4
Ready in 20 minutes

- 6 young dryad's saddle mushrooms, sliced thickly lengthways
- 25g/1oz/2 tbsp butter
- 5ml/1 tsp rapeseed oil
- 2 garlic cloves, sliced lengthways
- 5ml/1 tsp clear honey
- 200g/7oz mousserons
- 100g/3¾oz wild asparagus
- 1 hot red chilli, chopped
- 1 x 400g/14oz can chickpeas
- 1 red grapefruit, half juiced and half in chopped segments
- 5ml/1 tsp white wine vinegar
- 30g/2 tbsp chopped fresh flat leaf parsley
- 30g/2 tbsp chopped fresh dill, ripped into small pieces
- Handful of fresh mint leaves, torn if large
- 20g/¾oz violas or any other edible flower (optional)
- 45ml/3 tbsp natural (plain) yogurt
- Sea salt and black pepper
- Griddled pitta or crusty bread, to serve

1 Preheat the oven to 190°C/375°F/Gas 5 and preheat a griddle pan. Place the dryad's saddle slices on the griddle and cook for 2 minutes, then turn and cook for 1 minute. Do this in batches, if need be. Wrap in foil and bake in the oven for 10 minutes.

2 Meanwhile, in a frying pan, melt the butter and add the oil. Sauté the garlic for 30 seconds, stirring, then mix in the honey. Add the mousserons and sauté, continuing to stir and coat the mushrooms and garlic slices, for 2 minutes, until everything is golden. Transfer with a slotted spoon to a plate, then add the wild asparagus, chilli and chickpeas, pouring in half the grapefruit juice and all of the vinegar. Stir in the flat leaf parsley and cook for 2 minutes, then return the mousserons and garlic to the pan.

3 On a large serving plate, assemble the dryad's saddle, mousseron mixture, dill, mint, violas and grapefruit segments. In a small bowl, mix together the yogurt and remaining grapefruit juice, and season with salt and pepper. Dress the salad with the yogurt and serve with pitta breads or crusty bread.

PER SERVING: ENERGY 161KCAL/674KJ | PROTEIN 7.7G | CARBOHYDRATE 14.3G, OF WHICH SUGARS 4.6G | FAT 8.5G, OF WHICH SATURATES 3.7G | CHOLESTEROL 13MG | CALCIUM 77MG | FIBRE 6.3G | SODIUM 184MG.

A recipe that celebrates the chameleon nature of eryngii, this lobster, crème fraîche, lemon, dill and whiskey appetizer sees the sturdy mushroom take on the shape and texture of scallops, guaranteed to liven up your guests' palates. Eryngii mushrooms are very absorbent and so take on the juices of the lobster to make a very convincing fish. You can go for a peaty whiskey to give this dish a smoked feel, or a sweeter one for a more caramelized taste, but either way, this is a quick, simple yet impressive start to any summer meal.

Faux scallops and lobster in dill and lemon sauce

Serves 4 as an appetizer
Ready in 15 minutes

- 15g/½oz/1 tbsp butter
- 5ml/1 tsp olive oil
- 2 garlic cloves, crushed
- 2.5g/½ tsp sugar
- 4 eryngii, sliced
- 60ml/4 tbsp whiskey (see advice above)
- 1 cooked lobster tail, peeled and roughly chopped
- 45ml/3 tbsp crème fraîche
- 15g/1 tbsp chopped fresh dill, plus extra for garnish
- Zest and juice of ½ lemon
- Sea salt and black pepper
- Crusty bread, to serve

1 In a frying pan, heat the butter and oil, then sauté the garlic for 1 minute. Stir in the sugar, then add the mushrooms, frying, until golden for 2–3 minutes. Turn the heat up and add the whiskey, stirring and reducing for 2 minutes.

2 Add the lobster to the pan and stir-fry for 2 minutes, before adding the crème fraîche, dill and lemon zest and juice. Season to taste, then turn the heat down and simmer for 1 minute, or until the lobster is piping hot. Serve with crusty bread, and garnish with dill.

PER SERVING: ENERGY 144KCAL/596KJ | PROTEIN 6.8G | CARBOHYDRATE 0.5G, OF WHICH SUGARS 0.4G | FAT 9G, OF WHICH SATURATES 5.2G | CHOLESTEROL 48MG | CALCIUM 39MG | FIBRE 0.9G | SODIUM 111MG.

The mighty eryngii is one of our favourite cultivated mushrooms – it looks great however you prepare it, and its thick, sweet flesh is so versatile and malleable it can easily become the star of many a meal. In this recipe, it shares the limelight with succulent crab meat and the salty sea vegetable that is marsh samphire. The eryngii's extra-firm texture makes it a good companion to shellfish, highlighting the contrasting flavours. This is a good appetizer to make ahead, chill and then bake when needed.

Crab-stuffed eryngii

Serves 4
Ready in 30 minutes

Meat of 1 whole cooked crab (about 200–250g/7–9oz)
30ml/2 tbsp natural (plain) yogurt
Zest and juice of 1 lemon
15g/1 tbsp cornflour (cornstarch)
1 red chilli, sliced
45g/3 tbsp chopped fresh tarragon
4 eryngii mushrooms, halved lengthways
200g/7oz marsh samphire
15ml/1 tbsp white wine vinegar
Ground black pepper

Tip: If you have a whole crab to shell, first break open the crab by placing a clean dish towel around it, shell-side up, and then swiftly hit it in the middle with the end of a rolling pin. Crack the claws open and place the white flesh into a bowl, then add the grey and pink flesh from the main shell, discarding the shell, legs, soft feathery gills and stomach sack.

1 Preheat the oven to 200°C/400°F/Gas 6 and grease a baking sheet. In a bowl, mix the crab meat with the yogurt, half the lemon juice, cornflour, chilli and tarragon. Season with pepper.

2 Take each mushroom half, cut-side up, and carefully cut a line inside the edge and one cut down the middle of the insertion. Using a teaspoon, scoop out the mushroom flesh inside the insertion to make a deep hole. Place on the baking sheet and then fill with the crab mixture and season with pepper. Bake for 20 minutes.

3 Meanwhile, dress the samphire with the remaining lemon juice and zest and the vinegar. Divide between four plates and top each with two halves of the mushrooms. Serve.

PER SERVING: ENERGY 122KCAL/509KJ | PROTEIN 14.8G | CARBOHYDRATE 6.5G, OF WHICH SUGARS 1.8G | FAT 4.2G, OF WHICH SATURATES 0.6G | CHOLESTEROL 45MG | CALCIUM 53MG | FIBRE 2.2G | SODIUM 273MG.

A lot of people find slicing mushrooms therapeutic and the same can be said for making sushi, so we give to you 'therapy in a recipe' with mushroom sushi. Sushi-making is easier than you might think, and we'll take you through cooking and cooling the rice, rolling and decorating with soy-soaked chestnut mushrooms, bitter enoki and fish-like eryngii slices, and wrapping with nori (seaweed sheets). Once you master the technique you can use this recipe to make all kinds of different mushroom sushi. It's best to use raw cultivated mushrooms for this recipe, as their flavours make a natural partner for the sushi. There are four different pieces to make here, but if you make just one type simply increase the quantities of the ingredients you need.

Mushroom sushi

Makes 32 pieces
(6–8 pieces per portion)

- 1 eryngii, sliced lengthways
- ½ packet of enoki
- 4 chestnut mushrooms
- 30ml/2 tbsp soy sauce, plus extra to serve
- 100g/3¾oz any kind of shimeji, chopped roughly
- 500g/1¼lb sushi rice
- 125ml/4¼oz sushi vinegar/seasoning, plus 15ml/1 tbsp
- 15ml/1 tbsp wasabi, plus extra to serve
- 2 sheets of nori
- 50g/2oz black lumpfish caviar
- ¼ red (bell) pepper, sliced very thinly
- 4 chives, snipped
- ½ ripe firm avocado, chopped finely
- Sea salt
- Pickled ginger, to serve

1 In a large bowl, sprinkle the eryngii and enoki with a pinch of salt, then cover with cold water. Leave to soak. In another bowl, break the chestnut mushrooms into small pieces and dress with the soy sauce. Leave to soak. In a separate bowl again, place the shimeji and cover with boiling water. Stand for 2 minutes, then drain and refresh with cold water.

2 Rinse the rice with cold water, then place in a large pan and cover with 750ml/1¼ pint/3 cups of cold water. Cover with a lid, then bring to the boil and simmer, without stirring for 15 minutes or until all the water has completely evaporated. Add the vinegar, quickly mixing in a chopping motion to cover the rice completely, whilst it is hot. The rice should be very sticky and dense. On a baking sheet covered in lining paper, lay the rice out flat and fan with small chopping board, book or newspaper for 5 minutes or until the rice is cool.

> *Recipe continues overleaf*

PER PIECE: ENERGY 66KCAL/276KJ | PROTEIN 1.8G | CARBOHYDRATE 12.8G, OF WHICH SUGARS 0.3G | FAT 0.7G, OF WHICH SATURATES 0.1G | CHOLESTEROL 4MG | CALCIUM 5MG | FIBRE 0.5G | SODIUM 101MG.

3 In a small bowl, combine 15ml/1 tbsp of the vinegar with 100ml/3½fl oz/scant ½ cup of cold water. If the rice gets too sticky, you can dip your fingers into this to cleanse them. Lay out your rolling mat and transfer around three small handfuls of the rice to the centre of the mat. Place the end of the mat over the rice and roll it back to the end with a firm pressure, rolling the rice to the back of the mat. Roll it back and forth to make a sausage shape then roll it out of the mat. Separate the roll into two and then again to make four pieces.

4 Add a dab of wasabi to each piece of rolled rice and then a piece of rinsed eryngii on top. Snip 4 long thin strips of nori away from one of the sheets and dip in the water and vinegar mix quickly. Wrap around each sushi roll, then top with 2.5g/½ tsp of the caviar. Repeat steps 3 and 4 until you have 8 pieces of the eryngii sushi.

5 Repeat step 3 twice to make 8 plain rice pieces. Rinse the enoki and cut them to size then gather into 8 mounds and wrap the pepper strips around them to make little bundles, then set on top of the rice pieces. Garnish with the snipped chives. Make 8 more plain rice pieces following step 3 of the recipe. Cut the remaining nori into 8 thick strips, a little higher than the rice pieces. Dab the nori strips with a little of the vinegar and water mixture on the rough side, then wrap around the rice and hold together to fix. With a teaspoon, fill the tops with the chestnut mushroom mixture.

6 For the last type of sushi, mix the remaining rice in a bowl with the shimeji, avocado and remaining wasabi. Roll into hand-sized balls. Serve all the different types of sushi with extra soy sauce for dipping, wasabi and pickled ginger.

Inspired by a famous hotel in Belfast that likes to serve of a morning cereal with whiskey and cream, this breakfast is a decadent treat of extra-special mini girolle and flat mushrooms, both found commonly in Northern Ireland. The flat mushrooms are packed full of flavoursome black pudding, baked, then topped with a poached egg and girolles pan-fried in butter, whiskey and crème fraîche. It's finished off with blackberries and watercress to add fresh, tart tastes, as well as a few vitamins, amongst the indulgence.

The Belfast breakfast

Serves 2
Ready in 30 minutes

- 2 flat mushrooms, halved
- 100g/3¾oz black (blood) pudding
- 100g/3¾oz blackberries
- 3 garlic cloves, crushed
- 30g/2 tbsp chopped fresh curly parsley
- 50g/2oz/4 tbsp butter, softened
- 100g/3¾oz girolles
- 50ml/2fl oz/¼ cup whiskey (go for one with vanilla tones, if you can)
- 15g/1 tbsp wholegrain mustard
- 30g/2 tbsp crème fraîche
- Juice and zest of ½ lemon
- 100g/3¾oz watercress
- Ground black pepper
- Poached eggs and crusty bread, to serve

1 Preheat the oven to 180°C/350°F/Gas 4. Place the flat mushrooms on a baking sheet. Crumble the black pudding into a bowl, add 50g/2oz blackberries, garlic, parsley and 25g/2oz/2 tbsp of the butter. Stir and season with black pepper, then divide the mixture between the mushroom halves with your hands. Bake for 20 minutes.

2 In the meantime, melt the remaining 25g/2oz/2 tbsp butter in a frying pan and add the girolles, cooking for 2 minutes. Turn to a high heat and add the whiskey, stirring to reduce for 1 minute, then stir in the mustard and crème fraîche. Season with black pepper. Whiz up the remaining blackberries and all of the lemon juice and zest in a food processor or in a bowl with a fork.

3 Serve the baked mushrooms on a bed of watercress with a poached egg, drizzled with the girolles and blackberry purée, and serve with crusty bread.

PER SERVING: ENERGY 502KCAL/2079KJ | PROTEIN 11.7G | CARBOHYDRATE 12.2G, OF WHICH SUGARS 4.4G | FAT 39.4G, OF WHICH SATURATES 21.4G | CHOLESTEROL 92MG | CALCIUM 225MG | FIBRE 7.5G | SODIUM 732MG.

Again, putting Asian mushrooms in familiar surroundings, here we have a refreshing som tum, based on the traditional hot, sweet and sour Thai salad. The fresh and fragrant Thai flavours, lime, palm sugar and papaya, mix beautifully with the naturally sweet and crunchy, lightly blanched brown and white shimeji mushrooms. And the long, thin, but strong enoki act as a low-carb replacement for noodles – the clever little things.

Mushroom som tum

Serves 2
Ready in 15 minutes

150g/5oz green beans, trimmed
1 packet enoki, trimmed
2 packets white and brown shimeji, trimmed
2 garlic cloves, finely crushed
1 red chilli, shredded
1 green papaya, peeled and very finely sliced
150g/5oz cherry tomatoes, quartered
Small bunch of fresh coriander (cilantro) sprigs
15g/1 tbsp dried shrimp
Zest and juice of 2 limes
5g/1 tsp palm sugar
15ml/1 tbsp Thai fish sauce
15g/1 tbsp peanuts, crushed

1 In a large pan, place the green beans, enoki and shimeji and cover with boiling water. Cover with clear film or plastic wrap and stand for 5 minutes. Drain and refresh, then transfer to a large bowl. Add the garlic, chilli, papaya, tomatoes, coriander and shrimp, then toss thoroughly.

2 In a small bowl, mix together the lime zest and juice, sugar and fish sauce, then coat the salad with it. Transfer to a serving bowl, then sprinkle with the peanuts. Serve as an appetizer for four or a main for two.

PER SERVING: ENERGY 207KCAL/866KJ | PROTEIN 16.2G | CARBOHYDRATE 22.3G, OF WHICH SUGARS 8.1G | FAT 6.1G, OF WHICH SATURATES 1.2G | CHOLESTEROL 38MG | CALCIUM 241MG | FIBRE 12.1G | SODIUM 920MG.

Mushrooms can be so meaty that some people think a mushroom burger doesn't need actual meat. We are not amongst those people and have combined the best steak mince with some of the most interestingly textured mushrooms: portobello, oyster and eryngii. Using these cultivated mushrooms, you can have this burger at anytime, but we've added some golden summer girolles and tart blackberries to indicate that autumn is ahead, a teaser of the mushroom bounty that's to come. With a Camembert sauce and homemade onion rings, this burger is a treat and maybe not for the dieters…

Gourmet mushroom burger

Serves 2
Ready in 25 minutes, plus chilling

- 1 portobello mushroom, thinly sliced
- 300g/11oz minced (ground) steak
- 1 garlic clove, crushed
- 1 red chilli, chopped
- Pinch of sugar
- 1 egg, beaten
- 15g/1 tbsp chopped fresh curly parsley
- 100g/3¾oz oyster mushrooms, roughly chopped
- Plain (all-purpose) flour, for dusting
- ½ large onion, sliced into rings
- 1 eryngii, sliced
- 5g/1 tsp butter
- 50g/2oz girolles, ripped apart
- 50g/2oz Camembert cheese
- 100g/3¾oz blackberries
- 2 ciabatta rolls, halved diagonally
- 100g/3¾oz rocket (arugula)
- Sea salt and ground black pepper

Tip: To make a vegetarian alternative, replace the meat with the same weight of other minced mushrooms and add another egg to the mixture. Bake in the oven at 190°C/375°F/Gas 5 for 20 minutes instead of griddling.

1 In a pan, blanch the portobello mushrooms in boiling water for 5 minutes, then drain. In a large bowl, mix together the steak, garlic, chilli, sugar, beaten egg and parsley, then season. Roughly mix the oyster mushrooms into the meat mixture, then dust your hands with flour and shape into two patties. Place on a plate lined with baking parchment and wrap in with the portobello slices, then chill for 1 hour.

2 In the meantime, preheat the griddle and then cook the onion rings and eryngii slices for 2 minutes on each side. Place on a baking sheet, then keep warm on a low heat in the oven.

3 Cook the burgers for 3 minutes on each side, turning carefully to keep the mushrooms intact, for rare or to your liking on the griddle pan or in a frying pan, flipping once to cook evenly on each side. Meanwhile, heat the butter in a frying pan and add the girolle mushrooms, and fry for 2 minutes, until softened. Add the Camembert and when it has melted, stir in the blackberries. Toast the cut side of the ciabatta rolls under a preheated grill or broiler until golden.

4 Set up the ciabatta rolls on serving plates and place the rocket on the bottom piece. Top with the burger, onion rings and eryngii, then the girolle sauce, and the top of the bun. Serve immediately.

PER SERVING: ENERGY 575KCAL/2411KJ | PROTEIN 52.3G | CARBOHYDRATE 34.2G, OF WHICH SUGARS 8.2G | FAT 26.4G, OF WHICH SATURATES 11.2G | CHOLESTEROL 198MG | CALCIUM 292MG | FIBRE 9.1G | SODIUM 674MG.

Combining the tastes of both seasons as they change from summer to autumn, this cooling yet spicy shellfish terrine is light, creamy and refreshing. The rarely found lobster mushrooms are pan-fried then roasted to lock in their fish-like flavour and reinforce their spongy texture, which seems worlds apart from the delicate yellow oyster mushrooms. The orange pansies add a little velvety bitterness to this appetizer dish or decadent lunch – your guests won't believe it is made from mushrooms.

Crab and lobster mushroom terrine

Serves 4
Ready in 35 minutes

- 50g/2oz/4 tbsp butter
- 1 garlic clove, crushed
- 3 whole lobster mushrooms
- 1kg/2¼lb crab claws
- Zest and juice of 1 lemon
- 1 bunch of tarragon, roughly chopped
- 30g/2 tbsp natural (plain) yogurt, plus extra to serve
- 1 cucumber, ribboned
- 45g/3 tbsp chopped fresh dill
- 100g/3¾oz marsh samphire
- 100g/3¾oz small yellow oyster mushrooms
- 50ml/2fl oz/¼ cup white wine
- 5g/1 tsp chilli flakes
- Sea salt and ground black pepper
- Edible orange pansies, for garnish

1 Preheat the oven to 200°C/400°F/Gas 6. Melt the butter in a frying pan then add the garlic. Gently sauté for 2 minutes, then add the whole lobster mushrooms, braising for 2 minutes, turning occasionally. Remove the pan from the heat and transfer the mushrooms to a roasting pan, reserving the frying pan and garlic butter for later. Roast the mushrooms for 15 minutes.

2 In the meantime, crack the crab claws and remove the white meat, placing it in a bowl and discarding the shells. Mix in the lemon zest and juice, tarragon and yogurt. Season with salt and pepper, then chill. In a bowl, mix together the cucumber, dill and samphire, then season.

3 Chop the roasted lobster mushrooms roughly. Flash-fry the yellow oyster mushrooms in the reserved garlic butter in the frying pan for 2 minutes, add the wine and chilli flakes. Drain the cucumber mixture of its juices.

4 Place a cookie cutter on to a serving plate and fill with a quarter of the cucumber mixture. Leaving the cutter in place, top with a spoonful of the crab mixture and then some lobster mushroom pieces. Remove the cookie cutter and top with the extra yogurt and some of the oyster mushrooms. Repeat with the remaining ingredients to make four terrines, then garnish each with a pansy.

PER SERVING: ENERGY 322KCAL/1342KJ | PROTEIN 32.2G | CARBOHYDRATE 3.1G, OF WHICH SUGARS 1.4G | FAT 19.3G, OF WHICH SATURATES 7.7G | CHOLESTEROL 135MG | CALCIUM 71MG | FIBRE 1.5G | SODIUM 735MG.

Here we pair a mushroom that thinks it's shellfish with one of the sweetest, fleshiest fish around, monkfish. Packed with fresh flavours of lemon zest, garlic and basil, this courgette-wrapped fish, stuffed with chunky lobster mushroom pieces, is a simple, healthy supper that's bound to please.

Baked monkfish with lobster mushrooms

Serves 2
Ready in 40 minutes, plus chilling

- 400g/14oz piece of monkfish fillet, membrane removed
- 1 lobster mushroom, chopped finely
- Zest and juice of 1 lemon
- 1 garlic clove, sliced thinly
- 1 courgette (zucchini), trimmed and cut into strips lengthways with a vegetable peeler
- 15ml/1 tbsp olive oil
- Sea salt and ground black pepper
- Fresh basil, to serve

1 Preheat the oven to 200°C/400°F/Gas 6. Cut into the monkfish down the middle, lengthways, to create a cavity. In a small dish, combine the lobster mushroom, lemon zest and juice and garlic, then spoon the mixture into the monkfish cavity.

2 Lay out the clear film or plastic wrap on to a chopping board and then layer the courgette strips vertically on top. Place monkfish across the courgette strips, then wrap up tightly. Chill for 30 minutes.

3 Unwrap the monkfish and place on a baking sheet, then drizzle with the oil and season with salt and pepper. Bake for 25 minutes, until firm and white throughout. Slice and serve with the basil leaves.

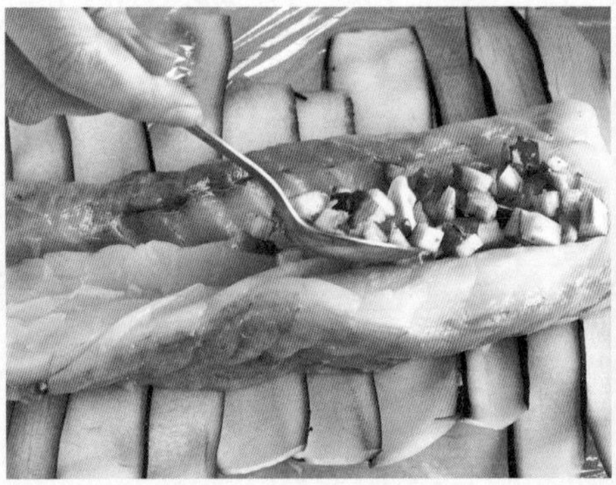

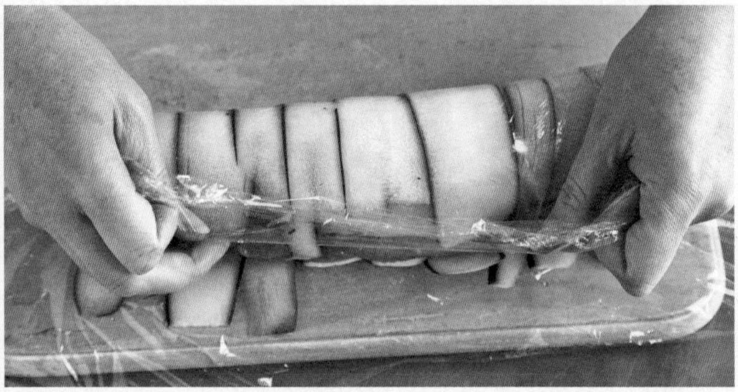

PER SERVING: ENERGY 209KCAL/883KJ | PROTEIN 34.6G | CARBOHYDRATE 2.1G, OF WHICH SUGARS 1.9G | FAT 7.1G, OF WHICH SATURATES 1.2G | CHOLESTEROL 28MG | CALCIUM 46MG | FIBRE 2.3G | SODIUM 41MG.

Growing up in a pickle-mad household, where if something wasn't going to be eaten it got preserved in someway, Liz was determined to combine two of her favourite things and make a mushroom piccalilli her mother would be proud of. Our piccalilli has all the usual summer vegetables you'll want to savour through to winter, as well as loads of wonderfully spongy cultivated mushrooms, which add a little bit of flavour but mostly soak up all the spices and that vinegar tang. This pickle is great with a cheese sandwich and turkey at Christmas time, or indeed with just about everything.

Mushroom piccalilli

Makes 1kg/2¼lb
Ready in 1 hour 25 minutes

- 1 packet enoki
- 3 eryngii, sliced
- 100g/3¾oz button (white) mushrooms
- 100g/3¾oz shiitake, sliced
- 2 packets of shimeji, 1 brown and 1 white
- 1 cauliflower, chopped into florets
- 3 courgettes (zucchini), sliced thinly
- 100g/3¾oz green beans, trimmed
- 3 green chillies, slit
- 1 red chilli, roughly sliced
- 1 red onion, quartered
- 1 solo garlic, quartered, or baby shallots, whole
- 30g/2 tbsp mustard seeds
- 30g/2 tbsp cumin seeds
- 30g/2 tbsp turmeric
- 30g/2 tbsp mustard powder
- 60g/2¼oz/generous ½ cup plain (all-purpose) flour
- 30ml/2 tbsp rapeseed oil
- 500ml/17fl oz/generous 2 cups white wine vinegar
- 100g/3¾oz/generous ½ cup sugar
- Sea salt

1 In a large bowl, mix together all the mushrooms, cauliflower florets, courgettes, beans, chillies, onion and garlic, and sprinkle liberally with sea salt. Cover with water and soak for 1 hour. Drain and rinse.

2 Mix together the mustard seeds, cumin seeds, turmeric, mustard powder and plain flour, then heat the oil in a large pan. Add the dry mixture and cook for 1 minute. Stir in the vinegar, 100ml/3½fl oz/scant ½ cup cold water and the sugar and bring to the boil. Add the rinsed vegetables and cook for 15 minutes, then store in sterilized jars.

3 The piccalilli will be ready to eat in 1 month and will keep unopened in a cool, dark place for up to 4 months. Once opened, keep chilled and eat within a week.

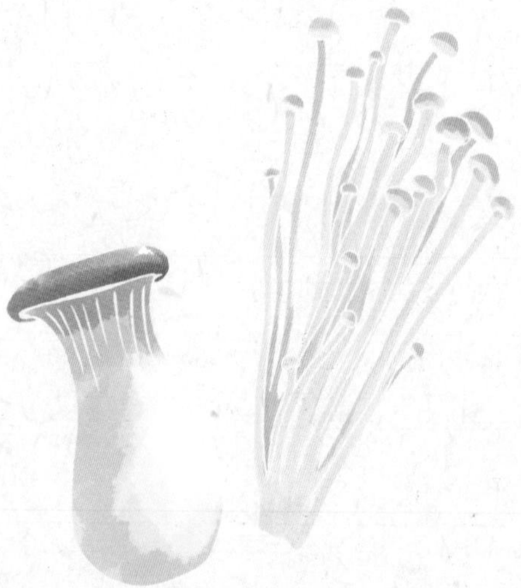

PER 1KG: ENERGY 1189KCAL/5002KJ | PROTEIN 67.1G | CARBOHYDRATE 189.7G, OF WHICH SUGARS 136.4G | FAT 54.3G, OF WHICH SATURATES 4.8G | CHOLESTEROL 0MG | CALCIUM 1595MG | FIBRE 32.1G | SODIUM 268MG.

There are some wonderful flavours in wild and cultivated mushrooms alike, and sometimes the best and easiest thing to do is throw them together with lots of garlic. In our tapenade, we have gone a little further and combined the smooth caramel tones of ceps, the sturdy chalkiness of pied bleu, the nuttiness of chestnut and umami of the shiitake, with olive oil, capers and anchovies to make a lively combination of flavours.

Mushroom tapenade

Serves 4
Ready in 12 minutes

- 60ml/4 tbsp olive oil
- 4 garlic cloves, peeled and bruised
- 50g/2oz chestnut mushrooms, chopped
- 50g/2oz shiitake, chopped
- 50g/2oz ceps, chopped
- 50g/2oz pied bleu, chopped
- 10g/2 tsp capers
- 2 anchovies
- Zest and juice of 1 lemon
- Black pepper
- Flatbreads or water biscuits, to serve

1 In a large frying pan, heat 15ml/1 tbsp oil and add the garlic, sautéing for 2 minutes. Stir in all the mushrooms and cook, stirring, for 10 minutes. Season with pepper and allow to cool.

2 Transfer the garlic and mushrooms to a food processor, then blend with the capers, anchovies, lemon zest and juice and remaining 45ml/3 tbsp oil. Chill for 20 minutes, then serve with flatbreads or water biscuits.

PER SERVING: ENERGY 115KCAL/472KJ | PROTEIN 1.8G | CARBOHYDRATE 1.2G, OF WHICH SUGARS 0.2G | FAT 11.4G, OF WHICH SATURATES 1.7G | CHOLESTEROL 1MG | CALCIUM 9MG | FIBRE 1.1G | SODIUM 62MG.

When really fresh, thinly sliced raw button mushrooms can taste of coconut, and wild ceps of chestnuts. This salad is very simple to put together, and a light, fresh citrusy dressing brings all the flavours to the forefront. Do try this with other mushrooms, especially truffle, if you can get your hands on it, but do double check the directory to see if you can eat the mushroom type raw first.

Raw mushroom salad

Serves 2

- 400g/14oz eryngii, ceps, flat and button (white) mushrooms, sliced and grated
- Juice and zest of 1 lemon
- 25ml/1½ tbsp truffle oil
- 15g/1 tbsp roughly torn fresh flat leaf parsley
- 15g/1 tbsp ground pink peppercorns
- Sea salt and ground black pepper

1 Combine all the mushrooms together and dress with the lemon zest and juice, truffle oil, parsley and pink peppercorns. Season with salt and pepper and divide between two plates. Serve.

PER SERVING: ENERGY 119KCAL/491KJ | PROTEIN 3.8G | CARBOHYDRATE 1.2G, OF WHICH SUGARS 0.7G | FAT 11.1G, OF WHICH SATURATES 1.7G | CHOLESTEROL 0MG | CALCIUM 23MG | FIBRE 3.3G | SODIUM 12MG.

AUTUMN

AUTUMN

Autumn is the season when the mushroom world comes alive with both wild and cultivated fungi in abundance. This is the time to get yourself down to the market and get experimenting in the kitchen.

This mushroom tempura is light, fluffy and wonderfully umami in taste – and such a great way to cook this crazy, coral-lookalike mushroom. If you can get your hands on a cauliflower mushroom it is a real treat, but it's rare, so do use other mushrooms in this recipe. Shiitake takes on both a wonderful texture and taste, and puffball sticks are perfectly squidgy inside. Mixed mushrooms can create a guessing game, for guests to discover the different mushrooms for themselves.

Tempura mushrooms

Serves 4
Ready in 45 minutes, including chilling

- 400g/14oz/3½ cups plain (all-purpose) flour, sifted, plus 30g/2 tbsp for coating
- 100g/3¾oz/scant 1 cup cornflour (cornstarch), sifted
- 30g/2 tbsp baking powder
- 200ml/7fl oz/scant 1 cup chilled sparkling water
- Juice and zest of 1 lime
- 3 spring onions (scallions), finely chopped
- 75ml/5 tbsp soy sauce
- 15ml/1 tbsp honey
- 1kg/2¼lb mixed cauliflower, shiitake and puffball mushrooms or any other mushrooms
- 15ml/1 tbsp chilli oil
- Vegetable oil, for deep frying
- Pinch of salt

1 To make the batter, gradually mix in a bowl the flour, cornflour, baking powder and water together with a pinch of salt and the lime zest together using a whisk, until the mixture is smooth. Chill for 20 minutes.

2 To make the dip, combine the spring onions, soy sauce and honey in a small pan and reduce over a low heat for 5–8 minutes until smooth and glossy. Pour into a dipping pot and set aside.

3 Squeeze the lime juice over the cauliflower mushroom and rip into bitesize pieces and place in a bowl. Drizzle the shiitake mushrooms with the chilli oil in a separate bowl. Chop the puffballs into sticks. Coat all mushrooms with the remaining 30g/2 tbsp flour.

4 Heat the oil in a wok to 180°C/350°F, ensuring the oil is deep enough to cover the mushrooms. Take the bowl of batter out of the refrigerator.

5 Dip the mushrooms in the batter with tongs or with two forks, before immediately adding them to the oil. Cook for 1–2 minutes, turn, and cook for a further 1–2 minutes or until the batter is lightly browned. It is best to do this in batches, so you don't overcrowd the wok. Remove with a slotted spoon and drain on kitchen paper to remove any excess oil then serve immediately, with the dip.

PER SERVING: ENERGY 720KCAL/3028KJ | PROTEIN 15.2G | CARBOHYDRATE 109.2G, OF WHICH SUGARS 6.5G | FAT 27.8G, OF WHICH SATURATES 3.4G | CHOLESTEROL 0MG | CALCIUM 250MG | FIBRE 8G | SODIUM 2250MG.

Autumn in a bowl, this soup brings to together the greats of the season – the prized chanterelle, shavings of the revered black truffle, and rich and thick chestnuts. The nutty and creamy dense soup is topped with pan-fried chanterelles and crisp and sweet truffle croûtons, making it almost too pretty to eat! Almost…

Chanterelle, black truffle and chestnut soup

Serves 4–6
Ready in 40 minutes

- 30ml/2 tbsp sunflower oil
- 15g/½oz/1 tbsp butter
- 1 onion, chopped finely
- 200g/7oz chanterelles
- 200g/7oz cooked chestnuts, crushed
- 1 large potato (about 200g/7oz), peeled and sliced
- 1 litre/1¾ pints/4 cups water
- 2 slices of crusty white bread, cubed
- 6 black truffle shavings
- 200ml/7fl oz/scant 1 cup crème fraîche, plus extra for garnish
- Sea salt and ground black pepper
- Fresh flat leaf parsley, for garnish

1 In a large pan, heat 15ml/1 tbsp of the oil and the butter, then add the onion. Sauté for 10 minutes, stirring regularly and adding a little water if it becomes dry. Add the chanterelles and sauté for a further 2 minutes. Remove a quarter of the chanterelles and set aside.

2 Add in the chestnuts and potato, then pour in the water and bring to the boil. Simmer for 20 minutes on a medium heat and season with salt and pepper. Allow to cool slightly, then liquidize in a food processor or with a hand-held blender, and return to the pan.

3 In the meantime, preheat the grill or broiler. Place the bread cubes in a bowl and drizzle with the remaining 15ml/1 tbsp oil and then crush and crumble over the truffle shavings, combining thoroughly. Tip on to a foil-lined grill pan and grill for 2 minutes, turning regularly with a fish slice.

4 Stir the crème fraîche into the soup and add the reserved whole chanterelles. Serve topped with the truffle croûtons and garnished with an extra drizzle of crème fraîche, and flat leaf parsley.

PER SERVING: ENERGY 292KCAL/1216KJ | PROTEIN 3.6G | CARBOHYDRATE 24.9G, OF WHICH SUGARS 5.2G | FAT 20.4G, OF WHICH SATURATES 11.1G | CHOLESTEROL 54MG | CALCIUM 55MG | FIBRE 3.4G | SODIUM 79MG.

Mushrooms are considered one of the best breakfast foods and they live up to their reputation in this sweet and savoury American classic. Mushrooms feature in both the thick pancake batter and the garnish, and the dish is even finished off with a truffle-oil syrup, just to get the mushroom message over loud and clear.

American-style mushroom pancakes

Serves 2–3
Ready in 30 minutes

- 100g/3¾oz/scant 1 cup plain (all-purpose) flour, sifted
- 5g/1 tsp baking powder
- 50ml/2fl oz/¼ cup milk
- 1 egg, beaten
- 50g/2oz/4 tbsp butter, melted
- 100g/3¾oz trompettes, ripped
- 1 packet of enoki, trimmed
- 25g/1oz shiitake, sliced
- 120g/4oz/8 tbsp golden caster (superfine) sugar
- 15ml/1 tbsp white truffle oil
- 6 rashers or strips of smoked streaky (fatty) bacon
- Ground black pepper

1 In a large bowl, whisk together the flour, baking powder, milk and egg, then slowly whisk in 25g/1oz/2 tbsp of the melted butter. Add two-thirds of all the mushrooms. Chill for 30 minutes.

2 In the meantime, to make the syrup, place the sugar in a small pan, cover with 65ml/2¼fl oz of cold water and add the truffle oil. Simmer until the sugar dissolves and then bring to the boil, simmering on a medium to high heat for 10-12 mintues or until the mixture thickens. Set aside.

3 Add 15g/½oz/1 tbsp of the melted butter to a frying pan or skillet and sauté the remaining mushrooms for 4 minutes. Add in the syrup for the last minute of cooking.

4 Grill or griddle the bacon rashers for 4 minutes, turning once, until crispy.

5 In a clean frying pan or skillet, heat the remaining 15g/½oz/1 tbsp butter and drop in two tablespoons of the pancake batter for each pancake. Fry for 2 minutes on both sides. You may have to do this in batches, depending on the size of your pan. You should make around 6-8 pancakes.

6 Serve the pancakes each topped with equal measures of sautéed mushrooms and crispy bacon, a drizzle of the mushroom oil, and sprinkled with black pepper.

PER SERVING: ENERGY 585KCAL/2452KJ | PROTEIN 14G | CARBOHYDRATE 69.6G, OF WHICH SUGARS 43.4G | FAT 29.8G, OF WHICH SATURATES 13.3G | CHOLESTEROL 127MG | CALCIUM 115MG | FIBRE 2.6G | SODIUM 841MG.

Autumn is the best time to bake a loaf. Warming, filling and full of taste, a flavoured bread can be a meal in itself, especially if there are some meaty mushrooms in it. We've used some visually startling black trompettes, nutty grated parsnip and sweet Parmesan, along with fragrant fresh thyme for this loaf, but we've also had success with a chanterelle, Manchego cheese and sherry combination, so make a few ingredient changes of your own and see what you come up with.

Trompette, parsnip and Parmesan loaf

Makes 1 loaf
Ready in 1 hour, plus proving

- 500g/1¼lb/scant 4½ cups strong flour, sifted, plus extra for dusting
- 2 parsnips, grated
- Pinch of sea salt
- 10g/2 tsp roughly ground pink peppercorns
- 7g/2½ tsp active dried yeast
- 250ml/8fl oz/1 cup warm water
- 25ml/1½ tbsp extra virgin olive oil
- 200g/7oz trompettes, pulled apart into small pieces
- 60g/4 tbsp fresh thyme leaves
- 50g/2oz Parmesan cheese, grated
- 5ml/1 tsp white truffle oil (optional)
- Ground black pepper

1 In a large bowl, combine the flour and grated parsnips and make a well in the middle with your fist. Add the salt, peppercorns and yeast to the well and then add 125ml/4fl oz/½ cup of the warm water and the olive oil. Stir together with a spatula, in a figure-of-eight motion, bringing the dough together and adding the remaining 125ml/4fl oz/½ cup water gradually to make a dry dough ball. You may not need all of the water.

2 Once in a ball, knead, by folding the dough into itself with one hand, continuously for 10 minutes. Leave in the bowl and cover with oiled clear film or plastic wrap, then stand in a warm place for 1 hour.

3 After 1 hour the dough should be twice its size. Knock the air out of the dough by punching it with your fist. Gently knead in all the mushrooms, thyme and Parmesan, then when all combined, knead in the truffle oil and season with pepper. Transfer on to a floured surface and shape into a loaf. Place in an oiled loaf tin or pan, then make a few slits on the top with a sharp knife, cover with oiled clear film, then stand in a warm place for 45 minutes.

4 Preheat the oven to 220°C/425°F/Gas 7 and bake for 20–25 minutes, until golden and risen, and the bottom is firm. Allow to cool slightly, then cool completely on a cooling rack.

PER LOAF: ENERGY 2304KCAL/9753KJ | PROTEIN 76.6G | CARBOHYDRATE 427.5G, OF WHICH SUGARS 25.4G | FAT 43.7G, OF WHICH SATURATES 14G | CHOLESTEROL 47MG | CALCIUM 1353MG | FIBRE 42G | SODIUM 436MG.

Here, the star of the show is the cep. When steamed with a squeeze of lemon juice, they go soft and fluffy and their umami flavour shines through. The pretty chanterelles are the support act, with some fresh, fragrant herbs highlighting their quintessentially sharp and creamy flavours. In a little reminder of summer before the winter months take hold, these Greek-inspired mushroom vine leaf parcels are quick, easy and great for buffet food.

Baked sea bass and cep parcels

Serves 6
Ready in 40 minutes

- 150g/5oz ceps, sliced
- 150g/5oz chanterelles
- 45g/3 tbsp roughly chopped fresh mint
- 30g/2 tbsp chopped fresh dill
- Zest and juice of 2 lemons
- 45ml/3 tbsp extra virgin olive oil, plus extra for greasing
- 5 caperberries, sliced, plus extra to garnish
- 18 vine leaves in brine, rinsed and drained, or 6 pieces of baking parchment
- 6 x 100g/3¾oz sea bass fillets
- 200ml/7fl oz/scant 1 cup Greek (US strained plain) yogurt
- 1 garlic clove, crushed
- Ground black pepper

1 Preheat the oven to 190°C/375°F/Gas 5. In a large bowl, combine the ceps, chanterelles, half the mint, half the dill, half the lemon zest and juice, the olive oil and the caperberries. Season with ground black pepper.

2 Place three vine leaves together in an overlapping fan on a chopping board and position a sea bass fillet in the middle. Top with a sixth of the mushroom mixture and wrap up. Place on a greased baking sheet and then repeat with the remaining vine leaves, fish and mushrooms. If you are using baking parchment instead, just loosely wrap up the fish and its filling into a parcel shape, by folding the edges in.

3 Bake for 20 minutes or until cooked thoroughly – you can check this by taking one parcel out of the oven and checking if the flesh of the fish is pure white and flakey.

4 In the meantime, combine the remaining herbs, lemon juice and zest, yogurt and garlic together, then serve spooned on top of the vine leaf parcels.

PER SERVING: ENERGY 207KCAL/861KJ | PROTEIN 22.6G | CARBOHYDRATE 2.5G, OF WHICH SUGARS 1.9G | FAT 11.8G, OF WHICH SATURATES 3.5G | CHOLESTEROL 86MG | CALCIUM 196MG | FIBRE 1G | SODIUM 95MG.

These boats celebrate all the wonder of the first flush of young caesar mushrooms. Taking influences from Italy and Spain, where these mushrooms are prized, the recipe sprinkles fine slices of raw caesar on to globe artichoke leaves, along with griddled crispy prosciutto and a sweet sherry dressing. Serve as canapés or group together in a dish for an appetizer or indulgent salad, and these chestnut-flavoured mushrooms will be the talk of the table. Remind your guests to just eat the fleshy and delicate end of the artichoke leaves and discard the tough ends.

Caesar mushroom and globe artichoke boats

Makes 20 canapés
Ready in 1 hour 20 minutes

- 1 large globe artichoke
- 8 slices of prosciutto
- 3 caesar mushrooms, sliced vertically very thinly
- 100g/3¾oz Brie, sliced very thinly into 20 slices
- Zest and juice of 1 lemon
- 50ml/2fl oz/¼ cup dry sherry
- 75ml/5 tbsp extra virgin olive oil
- Sea salt and ground black pepper
- Fresh basil leaves, to garnish

1 In a large pan, cover the artichoke with boiling water and bring to the boil. Cover and simmer on a high heat for 1 hour until the leaves easily pull away from the artichoke. Drain and chill slightly by refreshing under cold running water. Remove the choke or beard as some people call it – the inedible spiky fibres, which are quite obvious and protect the leaves and the heart. Pull all the leaves away and place on a serving plate, discarding the smaller, flimsy artichoke leaves. Cut the heart, which will be the small flat and round disc of flesh in the middle, attached to the stalk, into small pieces, and keep to one side in a bowl.

2 Heat a griddle pan or frying pan to high and cook the prosciutto for 5 minutes or until brittle. Blot on kitchen paper and then break into pieces. Set aside.

3 Set out 20 globe artichoke leaves on a serving plate, then pop a slice of caesar mushroom on each artichoke leaf, followed by a slice of Brie, then top each with a few prosciutto pieces.

4 Whisk together the lemon juice, sherry and oil, season with salt and pepper, and mix into the pieces of artichoke heart in the bowl. Spoon over the artichoke leaves, garnish with the basil leaves and the lemon zest and crumble the remaining mushroom slices over. Serve immediately.

PER CANAPÉ: ENERGY 58KCAL/241KJ | PROTEIN 2.7G | CARBOHYDRATE 0.3G, OF WHICH SUGARS 0.2G | FAT 4.9G, OF WHICH SATURATES 1.5G | CHOLESTEROL 5MG | CALCIUM 17MG | FIBRE 0.1G | SODIUM 131MG.

This warming dish is filling and creamy, and pairs mushrooms and fish together for a taste and texture amalgamation. The black fungus, with its seaweed-like texture and velvety taste, goes wonderfully well with some more usual seasonal forest favourites, ceps and girolles, and the soft and firm salmon, pollock and prawns.

Fish and mushroom pie

Serves 4–6
Ready in 1 hour

- 50g/2oz dried black fungus
- 300g/11oz Maris Piper potatoes, chopped
- 1 sweet potato, peeled and chopped
- 100ml/3½fl oz/scant ½ cup milk
- 30g/¼oz/2½ tbsp butter
- 15g/1 tbsp chopped fresh dill
- 15g/1 tbsp chopped fresh parsley
- 15g/1 tbsp chopped fresh tarragon
- Zest and juice of 1 lemon
- 15g/1 tbsp plain (all-purpose) flour
- 200g/7oz salmon, chopped
- 200g/7oz pollock, chopped
- 150g/5oz raw prawns (shrimp)
- Pinch of sugar
- 75g/3oz each girolles and ceps
- 100g/3¾oz button (white) mushrooms
- 15g/1 tbsp mini pickled peppers/pepper pearls' or capers
- 15g/1 tbsp creamed horseradish sauce
- 15ml/1 tbsp brandy
- 30ml/2 tbsp single (light) cream
- Smoked salt and ground black pepper

1 Soak the black fungus in a bowl of 100ml/3½fl oz/scant ½ cup boiling water for 15 minutes. Drain, reserving the liquid. Cut away and discard any hard pieces.

2 Preheat the oven to 180°C/350°F/Gas 4. In a large pan of cold water, bring the potatoes and sweet potato to the boil. Simmer for 12 minutes, until soft, then roughly mash with a tablespoon of the milk and a teaspoon of the butter. Mix in all the herbs, except half of the dill, and the lemon zest, then season with the smoked salt and pepper. Set aside.

3 In a large pan, melt 15g/½oz/1 tbsp of the remaining butter, then mix in the flour, stirring and cooking for 1 minute. Gradually pour in the remaining milk and the reserved mushroom soaking liquid. Add the salmon, pollock, prawns and sugar, and cook, covered with a lid, for 2 minutes. Stir in the girolles, ceps, black fungus and button mushrooms, then cook for a further 2 minutes. Stir in the remaining dill.

4 Mix in the pickled peppers, horseradish, brandy and cream, then season with pepper. Pour into an ovenproof dish and top with the mash, in flat individual blocks, like you might space out dumplings. Melt the remaining butter and brush the tops of the mash with it. Bake for 30 minutes, until the potato is golden and the fish is piping hot throughout. Serve.

PER SERVING: ENERGY 254KCAL/1066KJ | PROTEIN 22G | CARBOHYDRATE 17.4G, OF WHICH SUGARS 4G | FAT 10.6G, OF WHICH SATURATES 4.3G | CHOLESTEROL 112MG | CALCIUM 100MG | FIBRE 3.8G | SODIUM 170MG.

This herby roast salmon is a late summer feast for mushroom enthusiasts, with crispy samphire, delicate cucumber flowers and textured pied de mouton, girolles, ceps and button mushrooms. The salmon skin is coated with a zesty combination of basil, dill and mint, with our hero the black truffle – not only does this skin add a lovely taste to the dish, it locks in moisture, making sure all the salmon juices get taken in by the mushrooms.

Roast salmon with garlic pesto and truffle

Serves 6–8
Ready in 1 hour 30 minutes

- 1 head of garlic
- 60ml/4 tbsp olive oil, plus extra for greasing
- 6 black truffle shavings
- 30g/2 tbsp each fresh basil, dill and mint, plus extra for garnish
- Juice and zest of 1 lemon
- 1.5kg/3¾lb whole salmon, gutted and head removed
- 100g/3¾oz ceps, chopped
- 100g/3¾oz pied de mouton, chopped
- 100g/3¾oz button (white) mushrooms
- 1 fennel bulb, trimmed and quartered
- 150g/5oz marsh samphire or fine celery strips
- Sea salt and ground black pepper
- Cucumber flowers, for garnish

1 Preheat the oven to 180°C/350°F/Gas 4. Place the garlic on a baking sheet and drizzle with 15ml/1 tbsp of the olive oil. Roast for 15 minutes, until softened. Squeeze all of the garlic out of the skins into a food processor and add 30ml/2 tbsp more oil, the truffle shavings, half of all the herbs and the lemon juice. Process until smooth.

2 Place the salmon in a greased roasting pan and with a sharp knife, make three small cuts in the skin. Smooth half of the roast garlic and herb mixture over the salmon skin, then turn over.

3 In a bowl, mix together the ceps, pied de mouton, button mushrooms and fennel, and stir in the remaining 15ml/1 tbsp oil and half of the lemon zest. Season with sea salt and ground black pepper and the remaining fresh herbs. Fill the salmon cavity with the mushroom mixture and the samphire. Spread the top side of the fish using all of the remaining garlic and herb mixure, then cover the roasting pan loosely with foil.

4 Bake for 1 hour, then remove the foil and bake for a further 15 minutes or until the skin is crispy and the flesh falls apart. Serve, garnished with cucumber flowers, dill and remaining lemon zest, mint and basil.

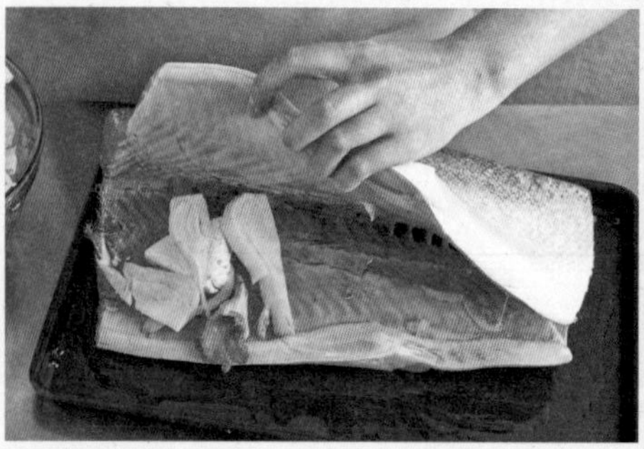

PER SERVING: ENERGY 393KCAL/1638KJ | PROTEIN 38.4G | CARBOHYDRATE 1.3G, OF WHICH SUGARS 0.6G | FAT 25.9G, OF WHICH SATURATES 4.8G | CHOLESTEROL 92MG | CALCIUM 83MG | FIBRE 1.5G | SODIUM 99MG.

Traditionally a popular pie filling because they were so cheap, oysters have had a radical image change over the last century. Now people prefer to eat them raw, but in these pies their soft cooked texture and metallic taste accentuates the delicate flavours of the woodland mushrooms. These pies are another opportunity to make hot crust pastry (see page 154 for the other recipe, mushroom pork pie); it's a joy to use with small pies but shape quickly as the hot pastry becomes less malleable as it cools.

Mushroom and oyster pies

Makes 6
Ready in 1 hour

10 oysters
20g/¾oz/1½ tbsp butter
1 garlic clove, chopped
8 girolles, halved
5 ceps, sliced
6 pied bleu, sliced
15g/1 tbsp cornflour (cornstarch)
200ml/7fl oz/scant 1 cup crème fraîche
50g/2oz marsh samphire
30g/2 tbsp chopped fresh dill
Zest and juice of ½ lemon
200g/7oz/scant 1 cup lard, chopped
500g/1¼lb/scant 4½ cups plain (all-purpose) flour, sifted
1 large egg yolk, beaten
Sea salt and ground white pepper

1 To prepare the oysters, wrap a clean dish towel around the middle of one, holding it flat-side up and with the join outwards. Holding the oyster over the dish towel, insert a short, strong, sharp knife into the end of the shell, where it joins. Dig in carefully and gradually, then lever the shells apart until the joint snaps. Lever the flat part up, then slice along the top inside to cut the oyster away from where it is attached. Discard the flat top, then run the knife underneath the oyster, along the curved bottom shell to remove it completely. Prepare the rest of the oysters in the same way.

2 Melt the butter in a large pan then add the garlic. Sauté for 2 minutes, then add the oysters and sauté for 1 minute. Mix in the girolles, ceps and pied bleu, then cook for 2 minutes. Mix in the cornflour and then stir in the crème fraîche, marsh samphire, dill and lemon zest and juice. Allow to cool.

3 Preheat the oven to 190°C/375°F/Gas 5. Cut out six circles of baking parchment, 15cm/6in in diameter.

> *Recipe continues overleaf*

PER SERVING: ENERGY 771KCAL/3215KJ | PROTEIN 12.3G | CARBOHYDRATE 68.7G, OF WHICH SUGARS 2.1G | FAT 51.6G, OF WHICH SATURATES 24.7G | CHOLESTEROL 124MG | CALCIUM 181MG | FIBRE 3.9G | SODIUM 167MG.

4 In a large pan, melt the lard in 200ml/7fl oz/scant 1 cup of boiling water on a medium heat. Place the flour in a large bowl and add a pinch of salt, then make a well in the middle of the dry mixture. Bring the lard and water up to the boil and then as it boils, pour it into the flour and mix quickly and thoroughly together with a wooden spoon. Keep stirring until you have an oily but smooth, golden dough. Set aside until the dough is cool enough to touch then knead in the bowl for 5 minutes.

5 On a floured surface, roll out the dough into a large rectangle to around $50cm^2/20in^2$, and with a pastry or cookie cutter, cut out four 10cm/4in circles. Place each circle of pastry on to a circle of baking parchment, then cut out five 8cm/1½in circles for lids. Roll out the cut-off pastry to make an additional large and small circle, placing the large one on the remaining parchment circle. Do this quickly as the dough will dry out and become less malleable as it cools.

6 Spoon about 2 heaped tablespoons of the oyster mixture on to one of the larger circles and bunch up the sides of the pastry to make a pie, pinching and shaping where necessary. Bring the baking parchment up around it, then secure by tying kitchen string around it and fixing with a box or knot. Top with a smaller circle of pastry, pinching the edge and sides together to secure. Repeat to make six pies.

7 Place the pies on a flat baking sheet and brush the pie tops with the egg. Bake for 25 minutes or until golden.

One of Michael's favourite recipes, this noodle dish – which is thought to originate in Japan, although it exists in many versions throughout Asia – makes good use of the multitude of cultivated mushrooms that are grown in abundance that side of the world. Served with slices of roast pork, a soft boiled egg, chilli oil and dried seaweed, this substantial noodle soup demonstrates to a tee both the beauty and texture of cultivated mushrooms.

Asian mushroom and pork ramen

Serves 4–6
Ready in 1 hour 45 minutes

- 700g/1⅔lb mini pork shoulder joint
- 15ml/1 tbsp soy sauce
- 3 garlic cloves, 1 crushed, 1 whole, 1 sliced
- 30ml/2 tbsp vegetable oil
- 30g/1¼oz mixed dried mushrooms
- 4–6 eggs
- 15g/1 tbsp Chinese five spice powder
- 10g/2 tsp chilli powder
- 10g/2 tsp palm sugar
- 5cm/2in piece of fresh root ginger, sliced
- 30ml/2 tbsp sake or rice vinegar
- 400g/14oz shimeji, enoki and nameko
- 2 eryngii and matsutake, sliced lengthways
- 300g/11oz straight-to-wok thin noodles
- 1 nori sheet, snipped into ribbons
- 2 spring onions (scallions), sliced
- 1 red chilli, chopped (optional)
- Ground white pepper

1 Preheat the oven to 230°C/450°F/Gas 8. Place the pork joint in a roasting pan and allow it to come to room temperature. In a small bowl, mix together the soy sauce and the crushed garlic with the oil, then coat the pork with the mixture. Roast for 30 minutes, then turn the oven down to 180°C/350°F/Gas 4 for a further hour. Let the pork stand for 20 minutes, then slice.

2 Meanwhile, place 1 litre/1¾ pints/4 cups of boiling water and the dried mushrooms in a large jug or pitcher and stand for 10 minutes. Place the eggs in a pan of boiling water and simmer for 4 minutes. Drain and refresh in cold water until the eggs are cool. Shell the eggs and set aide.

3 In a large pan, combine the rehydrated mushrooms and their stock, the Chinese five spice, chilli powder, palm sugar, sliced ginger and sake, as well as the whole garlic clove and season with white pepper. Bring to the boil, then add all of the mushrooms and simmer for 10 minutes. Stir in the noodles and simmer for 2 minutes.

4 Divide between four to six bowls and top with halved boiled eggs, the nori, spring onions, sliced garlic and chilli, if using. Serve.

PER SERVING: ENERGY 464KCAL/1955KJ | PROTEIN 42.5G | CARBOHYDRATE 40.6G, OF WHICH SUGARS 2G | FAT 15.9G, OF WHICH SATURATES 3.8G | CHOLESTEROL 305MG | CALCIUM 74MG | FIBRE 4.4G | SODIUM 346MG.

A warming supper or delicious appetizer, this mix of nutty and rich Jerusalem artichokes with delicate and textured cauliflower mushrooms and flavoursome portobello mushrooms will make a cold, autumn day a lot brighter. We've added a bit of toasted sesame oil and nutmeg for a smoky, spicy feel, and if you can't get hold of the elusive cauliflower mushroom, then replace with blanched and drained actual cauliflower.

Portobello and cauliflower mushroom bake

Serves 2
Ready in 25 minutes

- 2 portobello mushrooms
- 15ml/1 tbsp toasted sesame oil
- 100g/3¾oz cauliflower mushrooms, chopped
- 15g/1 tbsp finely chopped fresh flat leaf parsley, dill and mint, plus extra leaves to garnish
- 6 quail's eggs or 2 hen's eggs
- 300g/11oz Jerusalem artichokes, peeled and chopped
- 200ml/7fl oz/scant 1 cup whole (full-fat) milk
- 15g/1 tbsp freshly grated nutmeg
- ¼ black truffle, shavings to garnish (optional)
- Sea salt and ground black pepper

1 Preheat the oven to 190°C/375°F/Gas 5. Brush the portobello mushrooms with the oil and place them, cap sides down, on a baking sheet. Mix the chopped cauliflower mushrooms with the herbs, then divide among the portobello mushrooms. Crack quail's eggs into the cauliflower crevices or create a hole in each portobello mushroom for a hen egg and crack it in. Season and place on a baking sheet, then bake for 20 minutes.

2 Place the Jerusalem artichokes in a pan and cover with the milk. Bring to the boil and then simmer for 15 minutes, until soft and the milk is absorbed. Mash with the nutmeg and season with salt.

3 Divide the artichoke mash between two serving plates and sit a baked mushroom on each. Garnish with the extra herb leaves and black truffle shavings, if using, and serve.

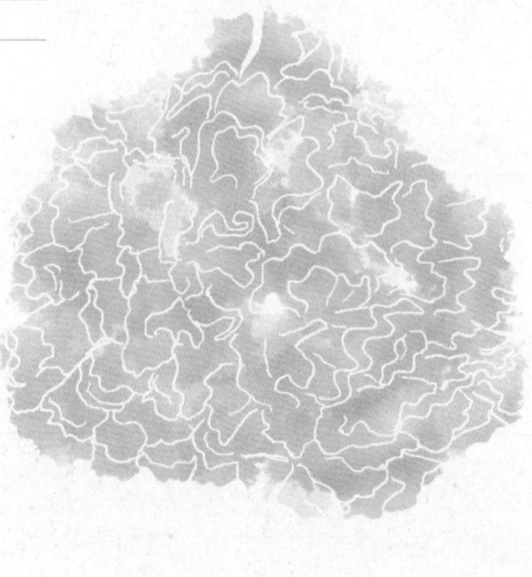

PER SERVING: ENERGY 280KCAL/1222KJ | PROTEIN 17.7G | CARBOHYDRATE 21.8G, OF WHICH SUGARS 7.8G | FAT 15.2G, OF WHICH SATURATES 4.1G | CHOLESTEROL 238MG | CALCIUM 205MG | FIBRE 10.7G | SODIUM 151MG.

Wild mushrooms with a good steak is a classic dish, and rightly so. The rich flavours of ceps, chanterelles, girolles and prized truffle amalgamate to accentuate the meaty, earthy tones of the good-quality fillet steaks we have used here. Add brandy and garlic to the mix, and you have the perfect meal for meat and mushroom lovers. We have used lightly poached cauliflower mushroom in this dish, and it adds an almost vegetable quality to the meal, but you can substitute with other mushrooms such as oyster or white enoki. This is lovely paired with a smooth yet dense red wine with notes of coconut, like a Rioja or Malbec.

Fillet steak with wild mushroom and truffle sauce

Serves 2
Ready in 20 minutes

- 1 cauliflower mushroom or 75g/3oz oyster mushrooms
- 30g/2 tbsp butter
- 15ml/1 tbsp olive oil
- 2 x 150g/5oz fillet steaks, at room temperature
- 100g/3¾oz ceps, quartered
- 40g/1½oz chanterelles
- 40g/1½oz girolles
- 2 garlic cloves, roughly chopped
- 25ml/1½ tbsp brandy
- 4 black truffle shavings
- 15g/1 tbsp finely chopped fresh curly parsley, plus extra to garnish
- Sea salt flowers (fleur de sel), ground black pepper and pink peppercorns

1 Place the cauliflower mushroom in a small pan and fill with boiling water. Simmer for 5 minutes, then refresh with cold water and drain. Tear the mushroom into bite-size pieces. If using oyster mushrooms, just add them in step 3 without blanching first.

2 In a non-stick frying pan, heat 15g/1 tbsp butter and all of the oil until sizzling. Place the fillet steaks in the pan, flat side down, and cook for 2 minutes, then turn and cook for 2 minutes for rare, longer if you prefer. Seal the edge in between the sides by picking the steak up with tongs and rolling it around the pan. Place the steaks on a warm plate and cover tightly with foil.

3 Turn the heat to low, then add the remaining 15g/1 tbsp butter and fry the ceps, chanterelles and girolles for 3 minutes, then add the garlic. Stir and cook for 2 minutes, then turn the heat up and add the cauliflower mushroom and brandy. Cook for 1 minute, then add the truffle shavings and parsley, and season with the salt flowers and pepper.

4 Transfer the steaks to serving plates and top with the mushroom mixture. Season with pink peppercorns and serve, garnished with parsley.

PER SERVING: ENERGY 421KCAL/1747KJ | PROTEIN 34.6G | CARBOHYDRATE 1.4G, OF WHICH SUGARS 0.4G | FAT 27.7G, OF WHICH SATURATES 13G | CHOLESTEROL 124MG | CALCIUM 18MG | FIBRE 2.2G | SODIUM 164MG.

Two of the great delicacies of nature, the mighty cep and tasty duck, join forces to make a Sunday roast with a diffference. Doused in red wine and blackberries, the duck is given a ruby-red glaze and packed full of a white truffle stuffing. White truffle is expensive and may seem a little flamboyant if it's not a special occasion, so white truffle oil (the foodie gift that keeps on giving) can be used instead. Adding another treat to this dish, the ceps are roasted whole, which makes them extra juicy and full of their own unique flavour.

Autumnal roast duck and ceps

Serves 4–6
Ready in 1 hour 20 minutes, plus resting

- 1.5kg/3¼lb whole prepared duck
- 400g/14oz blackberries, plus extra for garnish
- 250ml/8fl oz/1 cup red wine
- 25g/2oz/2 tbsp golden caster (superfine) sugar
- 15g/1 tbsp pink peppercorns
- 30ml/2 tbsp rapeseed oil, plus extra for greasing
- 1 head of garlic, broken into cloves, 1 clove crushed
- 200g/7oz pied bleu, half whole, half sliced
- 250g/9oz granary bread, chopped
- A few shavings white truffle or 15ml/ 1 tbsp of white truffle oil
- 30g/2 tbsp fresh flat leaf parsley, roughly chopped, plus extra to garnish
- 6 ceps, whole
- Sea salt and ground black pepper

1 Preheat the oven to 200°C/400°F/Gas 6 and place the duck in a greased roasting pan.

2 To make the glaze, put 200g/7oz blackberries in a pan with 150ml/¼ pint/⅔ cup of the red wine and sprinkle over the sugar. Simmer, without boiling, for 2–3 minutes, until the sugar has dissolved. Season with pink peppercorns and salt and pepper. Bring to the boil and hold on a rolling boil for 4 minutes until thickened. Allow to cool.

3 Heat a frying pan, then add 15ml/1 tbsp rapeseed oil. Sauté the garlic and sliced pied bleu for 2 minutes, then add the remaining 100ml/3½fl oz/⅓ cup red wine. Reduce for 1½ minutes, then add the chopped bread. Toss, continuing to cook, for 4 minutes, or until the bread is slightly toasted. Mix in the truffle or truffle oil, parsley and the remaining 200g/7oz blackberries. Stuff the duck cavity with the mixture and coat the duck skin with the blackberry glaze.

4 Roast the duck in the oven for 15 minutes, then lower the temperature to 180°C/350°F/Gas 4 and cover the duck loosely with foil. Roast for 20 minutes.

5 In the meantime, in a bowl, mix together the whole pied bleu and the ceps, and add the remaining 15ml/1 tbsp rapeseed oil and whole garlic cloves. Season and add to the roasting pan, surrounding the duck. Roast, covered in foil, for a further 25 minutes. Rest for 5 minutes, then serve, garnished with the extra blackberries and parsley.

PER SERVING: ENERGY 296KCAL/1244KJ | PROTEIN 19.4G | CARBOHYDRATE 27.9G, OF WHICH SUGARS 9.3G | FAT 9.6G, OF WHICH SATURATES 2G | CHOLESTEROL 75MG | CALCIUM 139MG | FIBRE 6G | SODIUM 313MG.

Inspired by Michael's travels to the Spanish coastal city of San Sebastian, this mushroom tapas is a simple yet effective way to enjoy individual mushrooms' unique flavours and textures. Considered the only way to eat wild mushrooms by some Spanish chefs, this is serious mushrooms on toast, with various different accompaniments, like soft grilled garlic, truffle shavings, lemon zest, parsley, pepper and sea salt, and quail's egg yolk. Mix the yolk into the hot mushrooms straightaway and add the flavouring you fancy – or just eat plain. You can use any wild mushrooms in this tapas, but we have chosen some of the best the autumn can offer from around the northern hemisphere.

Mushroom tapas

Serves 6–8
Ready in 15 minutes

- 8 slices of various breads or just one, including rye, sourdough and granary
- 60ml/4 tbsp light olive oil
- 3 ceps, sliced
- 1 matsutake, sliced
- 1 lobster mushroom, sliced
- 150g/5oz slice of puffball, chopped
- 100g/3¾oz grey and yellow chanterelles
- 4 garlic cloves, unpeeled and whole
- 8 quail's egg yolks
- 10g/2 tsp ground pink peppercorns
- ½ black truffle, shavings
- Zest of 1 lemon
- 30g/2 tbsp chopped fresh flat leaf parsley
- Sea salt and black pepper

1 Preheat the oven to 190°C/375°F/Gas 5 and preheat the grill or broiler. Place the bread on a baking sheet and drizzle with half of the oil. Place in the oven until needed.

2 On another baking sheet, place all of the mushrooms, making sure they are kept in their sections so they don't mix together, and add the garlic cloves. Drizzle with the remaining oil. Grill for 2 minutes and then turn the mushrooms over and grill for a further 2 minutes.

3 Top the bread with the different mushrooms and top each with a quail's egg yolk, then surround with the sea salt, black pepper, pink peppercorns, truffle shavings, lemon zest, grilled garlic and parsley. Serve.

PER SERVING: ENERGY 134KCAL/563KJ | PROTEIN 4.7G | CARBOHYDRATE 13G, OF WHICH SUGARS 1.2G | FAT 7.4G, OF WHICH SATURATES 1.3G | CHOLESTEROL 81MG | CALCIUM 70MG | FIBRE 2.6G | SODIUM 137MG.

Grilling mushrooms is a sure way to get the best out of their flavours. That's why we have taken some of autumnal forest floor's offerings and served them with some meaty lamb and pork chops, two sauces – one fiery, the other cooling – and some griddled herby potato cakes. Here we experiment with Spain's prized saffron milkcap, whole parasols, juicy ceps, tasty pied de mouton and fluffy puffballs, as part of a texture-filled sharing platter.

Mixed mushroom grill

Serves 4
Ready in 40 minutes

- 600g/1lb 6oz King Edward or floury potatoes, chopped
- 6 on-the-vine tomatoes, deseeded and chopped
- 2 Braeburn or robust apples, cored and chopped
- 1 garlic clove, crushed
- 1 red chilli, chopped
- 100ml/3½fl oz/scant ½ cup white wine vinegar
- 30g/2 tbsp caster (superfine) sugar
- 1 egg
- 15g/1 tbsp cornflour (cornstarch), plus extra for dusting
- Zest and juice of 1 lemon
- 60g/4 tbsp chopped fresh mint
- 30g/2 tbsp chopped fresh dill
- 4 pork chops
- 4 lamb chops
- 150g/5oz puffballs, chopped
- 4 parasols
- 4 pied de mouton
- 4 saffron milkcaps, stem cut off
- 6 ceps, halved lengthways
- 60ml/4 tbsp extra virgin olive oil
- 15g/1 tbsp capers
- Sea salt flowers (fleur de sal) and ground white peppercorns

1 Place the potatoes in a large pan and cover with cold water. Bring to the boil and simmer for 12 minutes. Drain and refresh under cold running water until cool. In the meantime, combine the tomatoes, apples, garlic, chilli, vinegar, sugar and 100ml/3½fl oz/scant ½ cup water in a pan and bring to the boil. Season with salt and white pepper, then simmer on a medium heat for 20 minutes. Transfer to a serving dish and keep warm.

2 Mash the potatoes roughly, then add the egg, cornflour, lemon zest and juice, 15g/1 tbsp mint and 15g/1 tbsp dill. Season with salt, then shape the mixture into four cakes, using the extra cornflour to dust and shape.

3 Preheat the griddle, grill or broiler and cook the pork chops and potato cakes for 5 minutes on both sides and the lamb chops for 3 minutes on both sides for rare. Keep warm, covered with foil, in a low oven.

4 In a bowl, combine all the mushrooms and coat with 30ml/2 tbsp oil, then season with salt and pepper. Add to a hot griddle pan or grill pan and cook for 4 minutes, turning occasionally. Sprinkle with the remaining 15g/1 tbsp dill.

5 In a food processor, whizz up the remaining 30ml/2 tbsp olive oil, the remaining 45g/3 tbsp mint and the capers. Arrange both sauces, the pork and lamb chops, the potato cakes and the mushrooms on a platter and serve.

PER SERVING: ENERGY 603KCAL/2529KJ | PROTEIN 48.5G | CARBOHYDRATE 41.7G, OF WHICH SUGARS 19.2G | FAT 28.1G, OF WHICH SATURATES 7.8G | CHOLESTEROL 243MG | CALCIUM 58MG | FIBRE 7.1G | SODIUM 167MG.

This is a great appetizer if you have been caught unawares by an impromptu dinner gathering. It can be made both well in advance or an hour or so before, so it's also easily portable. Using sweet woodland foraged mushrooms, mostly available at good markets in late summer and early autumn, this quick pâté makes the most of the delicate-tasting chanterelles and the more robust pied bleu and pied de mouton. If you're in a huge rush, you can use half chestnut mushrooms and half dehydrated and drained mixed or porcini/cep mushrooms.

Quick mushroom and sherry pâté

Serves 2–4
Ready in 15 minutes, plus cooling and chilling

- 25g/1oz/2 tbsp butter
- 400g/14oz ceps, pied bleu, pied de mouton and/or chestnut mushrooms, chopped
- 100g/3¾oz yellow and grey chanterelles, roughly torn apart
- 50g/2oz golden chanterelles, roughly torn apart
- 5g/1 tsp palm sugar
- Leaves from 1 sprig of fresh thyme
- 25ml/1¼ tbsp very dry sherry
- 50ml/2fl oz/¼ cup double (heavy) cream
- Zest of 1 lemon
- Sea salt and black pepper
- Crusty bread, to serve

1 In a pan or frying pan, melt the butter and sweat the ceps, pied bleu, pied de mouton and/or chestnut mushrooms for 5 minutes, then add all the chanterelles and sauté for 2 minutes. Sprinkle in the sugar and thyme and splash in the sherry, then cook on a high heat whilst stirring for 2 minutes, or until reduced. Allow the mixture to cool completely, and season with salt and pepper to taste.

2 In a food processor, blend the mixture until the desired texture is reached, then stir in the cream and lemon zest. Transfer to ramekins and chill for 15 minutes. Serve with crusty bread.

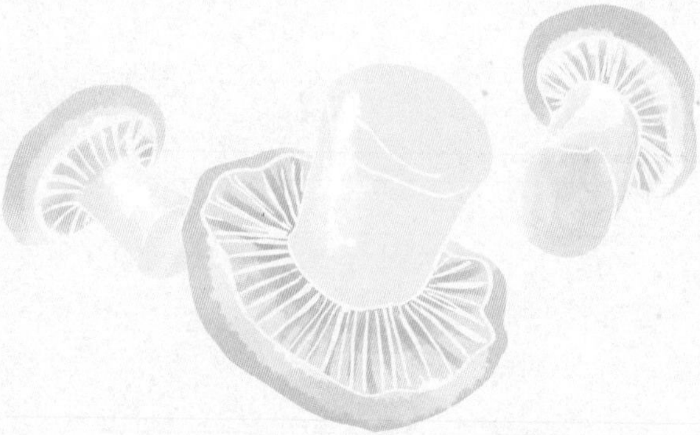

PER SERVING: ENERGY 138KCAL/569KJ | PROTEIN 2.7G | CARBOHYDRATE 1.9G, OF WHICH SUGARS 1.7G | FAT 12.6G, OF WHICH SATURATES 7.6G | CHOLESTEROL 30MG | CALCIUM 16MG | FIBRE 2G | SODIUM 48MG.

WINTER

WINTER

As other seasonal ingredients calm down to rejuvenate in wintertime, different wild as well as cultivated mushrooms from around the world are available to bring warming dishes to our tables.

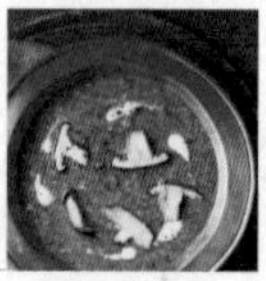

Seasonal late-autumn to early winter mushrooms, such as trompettes, pied de mouton and chanterelles, are a great natural pairing for most game, and partridge is no exception. The bird's subtle rich flavours complement the forest-like taste of these three mushrooms, with mousserons coming along to add a stronger morsel every other bite. The black pudding dumplings also add a hit of meaty flavour, accentuated with the thyme and orange, in this comforting winter warmer.

Partridge stew with black pudding

Serves 4–6
Ready in 1 hour 40 minutes

- 2 prepared partridges
- 75g/3oz/⅔ cup plain (all-purpose) flour
- 2 garlic cloves, chopped
- 15g/1 tbsp dried chilli flakes
- 15g/1 tbsp pink peppercorns
- Zest and juice of 1 orange
- 15g/1 tbsp cumin seeds, ground
- 30ml/2 tbsp rapeseed oil
- 500g/1¼lb banana shallots, quartered
- 100g/3¾oz pied de mouton
- 150g/5oz baby parsnips
- 150ml/¼ pint/⅔ cup white wine
- 15ml/1 tbsp Worcestershire sauce
- 750ml/1¼ pints/3 cups mushroom stock (see page 228)
- 45g/3 tbsp thyme leaves, plus extra sprigs for garnish
- 250g/9oz black (blood) pudding
- 250g/9oz/2¼ cups self-raising (self-rising) flour, plus extra for dusting
- 100g/3¾oz suet (US chilled, grated shortening)
- 100g/3¾oz yellow chanterelles
- 200g/7oz kale, roughly chopped
- 100g/3¾oz mousserons
- 100g/3¾oz trompettes
- Sea salt and ground black pepper

1 Chop the partridges into quarters. In a bowl mix together the flour, garlic, chilli, pink peppercorns, orange zest, cumin seeds and seasoning, and use to coat the partridge pieces. In a large pan, heat the oil and add the partridge quarters, sear for 4 minutes, until golden. Remove the partridges from the pan with a slotted spoon, retaining the oil in the pan.

2 Add the shallots and fry for 5 minutes, until golden. Add the pied de mouton and baby parsnips, and sauté for 2 minutes. Pour in the white wine and orange juice, and simmer for 5 minutes. Season, add the Worcestershire sauce and mushroom stock, as well as the thyme. Bring to the boil and add the partridges, then cover and simmer for 1 hour.

3 In a large bowl, mash the black pudding with the back of a fork until soft and crumbly and add the self-raising flour and suet, and seasoning. Pour in 30ml/2 tbsp cold water and add the chanterelles. Shape into eight dumplings, with hands dusted with flour. Add the kale, mousserons and trompettes to the stew, then the dumplings, cover and simmer for 20 minutes. Serve, garnished with extra thyme.

PER SERVING: ENERGY 729KCAL/3052KJ | PROTEIN 50.6G | CARBOHYDRATE 50.2G, OF WHICH SUGARS 7.4G | FAT 35.9G, OF WHICH SATURATES 14G | CHOLESTEROL 32MG | CALCIUM 285MG | FIBRE 5.9G | SODIUM 645MG.

Inspired by cold days in Copenhagen where open sandwiches not only warm you up but are pretty much a work of art, this creation has all the Scandinavian flavours you might hope for. We have used two cultivated mushrooms, oysters and the eryngii, for effect, texture (and height!) and because of their availability through the winter. Scandinavia is traditionally a mushroom-foraging region and flavours used in the cuisine lend themselves well to many different mushrooms, so do experiment with this open sandwich earlier in the year.

Open rare beef and mushroom sandwich

Serves 2
Ready in 40 minutes

- 5g/1 tsp Chinese five spice powder
- 45ml/3 tbsp olive oil
- 400g/14oz ribeye steak, at room temperature
- 1 garlic clove, halved
- 100g/3¾oz mixed oyster mushrooms, roughly torn
- Zest and juice of 1 lemon
- 1 eryngii, sliced
- 2 slices of sourdough bread
- 7g/2½ tsp fresh dill, chopped, plus extra for garnish
- 15ml/1 tbsp horseradish cream
- 30ml/2 tbsp sour cream
- Handful of rocket (arugula)
- 2 large gherkins, sliced into strips
- Sea salt and ground black pepper

1 Preheat the oven to 180°C/350°F/Gas 4. In a small bowl, combine the five spice powder, 15ml/1 tbsp olive oil and pinch of both the salt and pepper. On a roasting pan with a wire rack, place the steak and coat it with the spicy oil mixture. Place the pan in the oven and turn to 110°C/225°F/Gas ¼. Cook for 20 minutes, allow to cool for 10 minutes, then slice the steak.

2 Meanwhile, in a frying pan, heat 15ml/1 tbsp of the oil and add the garlic clove, to flavour the oil. Add the oyster mushrooms and stir-fry for 2 minutes, then add half of the lemon juice. Cover with a lid and cook for 2 minutes. Set aside with the lid still on, discarding the garlic clove.

3 Preheat the griddle pan and add the sliced eryngii, cooking for 1–2 minutes on each side, until charred. Set aside, then brush the bread with the remaining 15ml/1 tbsp oil. Fry the bread on both sides for 1 minute in the griddle pan, then place on serving plates.

4 In a small bowl, mix together the lemon zest, remaining lemon juice, dill, horseradish and sour cream, then season with pepper. Top the griddled bread slices with the rocket, sliced ribeye and mushrooms, then dress with the sour cream mixture and the gherkins. Serve, garnished with dill.

PER SERVING: ENERGY 532KCAL/2221KJ | PROTEIN 50G | CARBOHYDRATE 16.8G, OF WHICH SUGARS 3.1G | FAT 29.8G, OF WHICH SATURATES 8.1G | CHOLESTEROL 126MG | CALCIUM 98MG | FIBRE 3.2G | SODIUM 471MG.

Packed with nutrients and powerful flavours, this superhero of soups has the full house of vitamins – A, B, C and D! As well as setting you up for the winter months, the soup has a vibrant green colour and strong nutty, smoky taste, brought on by smoked salt, walnut oil and dry-fried kale. It is smart enough to wow any dinner party, but simple enough for a cosy night in.

Kale and shiitake soup

Serves 4
Ready in 45 minutes

- 16 shiitake
- 200g/7oz shallots, halved
- 4 garlic cloves
- 30ml/2 tbsp walnut or butternut squash oil
- 600g/1lb 6oz kale, rinsed and roughly chopped
- 1 litre/1¾ pints/4 cups mushroom stock (see tip below)
- Juice of ½ lemon
- 2.5g/½ tsp sugar
- Smoked sea salt and cracked pink peppercorns
- Sour cream and crusty bread, to serve

Tip: To make mushroom stock, place 400g/14oz dried mushrooms in a bowl and cover with 1 litre/1¾ pints/4 cups boiling water. Leave to soak for 15 minutes. Drain and reserve the rehydrated mushrooms to be used in another recipe. Reduce or enlarge quantities as required.

1 Preheat the oven to 190°C/375°F/Gas 5. On a baking sheet, place the shiitake mushrooms, shallots and garlic cloves and sprinkle over the walnut oil. Season with the salt and roast for 15–20 minutes, until the shallots are softened.

2 In the meantime, in a large pan, dry-fry the kale, in batches if needed, until the kale is moist and softened.

3 Add the roasted shallots and its juices to the kale, then peel the roasted garlic and add to the mixture. Add 4 shiitake mushrooms, then simmer, stirring, for 2 minutes. Slice the remaining 12 roasted shiitake and set aside.

4 Pour the stock into the pan and add the lemon juice and sugar, then bring to the boil. Simmer for 15 minutes, then allow to cool slightly, before liquidizing, in batches if necessary. Return the liquidized soup to the pan, then add the sliced shiitake mushrooms and pink peppercorns. Simmer for 2 minutes, then serve with a swirl of sour cream and crusty bread.

PER SERVING: ENERGY 116KCAL/484KJ | PROTEIN 6.8G | CARBOHYDRATE 4G, OF WHICH SUGARS 3.7G | FAT 8.3G, OF WHICH SATURATES 0.9G | CHOLESTEROL 0MG | CALCIUM 210MG | FIBRE 7.9G | SODIUM 72MG.

Mushrooms are a classic ingredient in Chinese cuisine. With this curry, we highlight the many different types of cultivated mushrooms you can get. From eryngii to enoki, shimeji to shiitake, all the different mushrooms add something to this dish, whether it's taste, texture or visual. You can use any kind of cultivated mushrooms here, just add the larger mushrooms first and the more delicate ones to the end. Of course, it is fine to use just one type, but where would the fun be in that? Go foraging in the farmers' markets or supermarkets and see how many kinds you can find... Steamed rice is the perfect accompaniment for this curry.

Chinese mixed mushroom curry

Serves 4
Ready in 1 hour

- 10g/2 tsp turmeric
- 10g/2 tsp coriander seeds, freshly ground
- 2 red chillies, chopped
- 5g/1 tsp ground cumin
- 30g/2 tbsp grated fresh root ginger
- 10g/2 tsp fenugreek seeds
- 15g/1 tbsp mild curry powder
- 2.5g/½ tsp sugar
- 15ml/1 tbsp solid coconut oil
- 4 garlic cloves, sliced
- 2 onions, quartered
- 2 portobello mushrooms, quartered
- 400g/14oz horse, button (white) and/or chestnut mushrooms
- 30g/2 tbsp cornflour (cornstarch)
- 50ml/2fl oz/¼ cup sherry
- 15ml/1 tbsp soy sauce
- 300ml/½ pint/1¼ cups mushroom stock (see page 228)
- 1 pack enoki, separated
- 1 pack brown shimeji, separated
- 2 eryngii, sliced lengthways
- 200g/7oz mangetouts (snow peas)
- 2 carrots, peeled and shaved
- 2 bulbs of pak choi (bok choy)

1 In a small bowl, combine the turmeric, coriander, chillies, cumin, ginger, fenugreek, curry powder and sugar. In a wok or large pan, heat the coconut oil until it melts, then add the spice mixture, and stir-fry for 1 minute. Turn the heat down and add the garlic and onions, coating completely with the spice mixture, and cook for 5 minutes, adding a little cold water if the pan becomes dry.

2 Turn the heat to a simmer, add the portobello, button, chestnut and horse mushrooms and 30ml/2 tbsp cold water, and cook, stirring for 5 minutes. In a small pot, jug or pitcher, blend the cornflour with the sherry and soy sauce, and add it to the wok. Add half of the stock, stir, then cover and simmer for 20 minutes.

3 Add all the remaining mushrooms, the mangetout and carrot, as well as the remaining half of the stock. Simmer, covered, for 10 minutes, then add the pak choi and simmer, uncovered for a further 10 minutes. Serve.

PER SERVING: ENERGY 202KCAL/847KJ | PROTEIN 9.5G | CARBOHYDRATE 25.3G, OF WHICH SUGARS 11.1G | FAT 6.2G, OF WHICH SATURATES 2.7G | CHOLESTEROL 0MG | CALCIUM 178MG | FIBRE 13.3G | SODIUM 376MG.

Soft, creamy and brilliantly green, these sweet Japanese green tea breakfast rolls perfectly complement the sweet taste of Asian enoki mushrooms. Made using a hot water-roux paste, the bread is smooth and fluffy as a result. As soon as the buns were out of the oven, we couldn't stop eating them – thankfully, all the antioxidants in green tea make them quite good for you.

Enoki green tea buns

Makes 16 large or 24 small buns
Ready in 45 minutes, plus proving

- 400g/14oz/3½ cups strong flour, sifted
- 80g/3oz/⅔ cup plain (all-purpose) flour, sifted, plus extra for dusting
- 20g/¾oz matcha green tea powder
- 30g/1¼oz coconut milk powder
- Pinch of salt
- 75g/3oz/6 tbsp caster (superfine) sugar
- 200g/7oz enoki, trimmed and separated
- 7g/2½ tsp active dried yeast
- 2 eggs, beaten
- 40g/1½oz/3¼ tbsp butter, plus extra for greasing
- Sunflower oil, for oiling

1 To make the water-roux paste, in a pan combine 25g/1oz/¼ cup of the strong flour with 125ml/4fl oz/½ cup cold water to make a paste. Place on the heat and simmer, whisking as you go to make a thick and glossy mixture. When thick, take off the heat and cover with clear film or plastic wrap and cool to room temperature.

2 In a large bowl, mix together the remaining strong flour, the plain flour, green tea powder, coconut milk powder, salt and sugar, then add the enoki mushrooms. Make a well in the middle of the mixture, then add the yeast, one of the eggs and the water-roux paste into it. Mix in a figure-of-eight to combine, gradually adding warm water a couple of tablespoons at a time, until a dough.

3 Transfer to a clean kitchen surface, lightly dusted with flour, and knead the dough quickly and keenly for 10 minutes. Knead the butter into the dough, then place in a large bowl and cover with oiled clear film and a damp, clean dish towel. Stand to prove for 1 hour.

> *Recipe continues overleaf*

PER LARGE BUN: ENERGY 158KCAL/667KJ | PROTEIN 4.4G | CARBOHYDRATE 29.2G, OF WHICH SUGARS 6.3G | FAT 3.4G, OF WHICH SATURATES 1.7G | CHOLESTEROL 35MG | CALCIUM 71MG | FIBRE 1.2G | SODIUM 38MG.

4 Knock back the dough, by punching the air out with your fist, then divide into 16 large or 24 small balls. Grease a baking sheet. Place the dough balls in lines, a little apart, on the baking sheet and cover with oiled clear film and a damp dish towel, and leave to stand somewhere warm to prove again for 45 minutes.

5 Preheat the oven to 190°C/375°F/Gas 5. Brush the buns with the remaining beaten egg and bake for 15 minutes, until risen and golden. Serve immediately or keep in an airtight container for up to a week. The buns are best eaten warmed.

Trompette mushrooms have an amazing dark brown, almost black, colour that not only looks great on a plate, but brings an extra boost in mushroom flavour. The wild mushroom's brittle texture is perfect for putting into a pasta dough as it's not too moist and the dough still holds together. We make this pasta with a pasta machine, but you could give it a go rolling it very thinly with extra semolina if you don't have one. Dressed with orange, thyme, Parmesan and pistachio nuts, this mushroom and garlic pasta shows off the trompettes' versatility.

Trompette pesto pasta

Serves 4
Ready in 30 minutes

- 300g/11oz trompettes
- 1 garlic clove, crushed
- 30ml/2 tbsp extra virgin olive oil
- 400g/14oz/3½ cups plain (all-purpose) flour, sifted
- 3 eggs, beaten
- 30g/2 tbsp semolina, to dust
- Zest and juice of 1 orange
- 60g/4 tbsp fresh thyme leaves
- 50g/2oz Parmesan cheese shavings
- 15g/1 tbsp crushed pistachio nuts
- Sea salt and pink peppercorns

1 In a food processor, whizz the mushrooms and garlic with 15ml/1 tbsp of the oil into a paste. Place the flour in a large bowl and make a well in the middle and pour the beaten eggs and the trompette mixture into it.

2 Using a fork, whisk the flour into the egg mixture from the outside in, until the mixture comes together, then shape into a ball with your hands. On a lightly floured surface, knead the dough for 10 minutes until firm and glossy. Divide the dough into eight pieces and wrap all but one in clear film or plastic wrap.

3 Roll the first piece of dough into a rectangle that will fit into the pasta machine and dust with semolina. Set the machine to the third-thinnest setting. Feed the pasta through the machine twice, dusting with semolina as you go. Change the setting to the second-thinnest setting and feed the pasta through once, then again on the thinnest setting. With a sharp knife, slice into strips, then lay on baking parchment and cover with a clean, damp dish towel. Repeat with the remaining pasta balls, layering each batch with a sheet of baking parchment.

4 In a large pan, cook the pasta in boiling water for 3–5 minutes, drain and refresh. Coat the pasta with the remaining 15ml/1 tbsp olive oil, orange zest and juice, thyme, Parmesan and crushed pistachio nuts, and season with salt and crushed pink peppercorns. Divide between warmed plates and serve immediately.

PER SERVING: ENERGY 573KCAL/2417KJ | PROTEIN 22.4G | CARBOHYDRATE 85.3G, OF WHICH SUGARS 3.1G | FAT 18.2G, OF WHICH SATURATES 5.2G | CHOLESTEROL 185MG | CALCIUM 305MG | FIBRE 5.8G | SODIUM 186MG.

Making the most of the amazing flavour that comes out of dried mushrooms when they are hydrated, this mushroom and Brie cheese soufflé is full of strong, earthy flavours with a delicate, light texture. Serve immediately to achieve the best results, although soufflés will always deflate on the walk to the dinner table. The good news is, they taste great either way!

Mushroom soufflé

Makes 4
Ready in 45 minutes

- 150g/5oz dried ceps
- 50g/2oz/¼ cup butter, plus extra for greasing
- 50g/2oz breadcrumbs
- 50g/2oz/½ cup plain (all-purpose) flour
- 300ml/½ pint/1¼ cups milk
- 100g/3¾oz Brie, roughly chopped
- 4 eggs, separated
- 30g/2 tbsp fresh thyme leaves
- Ground black pepper

1 Place the dried mushrooms in a bowl, pour in around 200ml/7fl oz/scant 1 cup of boiling water or until the mushrooms are totally covered and stand for 10 minutes. Drain, reserving 10ml/2 tsp of the mushroom stock (use the remaining stock for another recipe). Preheat the oven to 200°C/400°F/Gas 6 and grease four ramekins and coat with the breadcrumbs.

2 Melt the butter in a large pan and add the flour, stirring and cooking for 1 minute. Stir in the milk slowly and add the mushrooms, along with the reserved liquid. Simmer, stirring, until thickened and then stir in half of the Brie. Whisk the egg yolks and slowly mix into the flour mixture, then add the thyme and pepper.

3 In a separate, clean bowl whisk the egg whites with an electric whisk until completely firm. Fold into the flour and cheese mixture.

4 Pour the mixture into the ramekins and top with the remaining Brie. Run a flat knife around the edge of the mixture in each ramekin. Bake for 30 minutes, until risen and golden. Serve.

PER SOUFFLÉ: ENERGY 450KCAL/1880KJ | PROTEIN 25.9G | CARBOHYDRATE 25G, OF WHICH SUGARS 5.6G | FAT 28.1G, OF WHICH SATURATES 14.3G | CHOLESTEROL 286MG | CALCIUM 244MG | FIBRE 7.5G | SODIUM 454MG.

It's hard to beat a classic stuffed mushroom as an appetizer or lunch, so here's our version, using the faithful nutty and firm portobello, and packed with garlic. We've also upped the ante with the addition of a white truffle oil-infused aioli, that you can make with or without the truffle, if you prefer.

Stuffed portobello mushrooms with truffle aioli

Serves 4
Ready in 40 minutes

- 3 egg yolks
- 150ml/¼ pint/⅔ cup rapeseed oil
- 15ml/1 tbsp truffle oil
- Zest and juice of 1 lemon, plus extra wedges to serve
- 8 portobello mushrooms
- 5 garlic cloves
- 100g/3¾oz granary bread
- 100g/3¾oz/scant ½ cup butter, softened
- 60g/4 tbsp fresh flat leaf parsley, roughly chopped
- Salt and ground black pepper

1 In a large bowl, whisk the egg yolks with an electric whisk until light and fluffy. Add 5ml/1 tsp of the rapeseed oil and whisk together, then add another teaspoon. Whisk until it starts to thicken and looks creamy, then slowly add the remaining oil and truffle oil, whisking continuously. When thick, mix in a pinch of the lemon zest and 5ml/1 tsp of the lemon juice, then season with salt and pepper. Cover and chill until needed.

2 Preheat the oven to 200°C/400°F/Gas 6. Wipe the portobello mushrooms clean with damp kitchen paper and remove the stalks with a teaspoon. Place the stalks in a food processor, along with the garlic and bread, then whizz up into small pieces. Transfer this mixture to a bowl, then add the butter, the remaining lemon juice and zest and the parsley, and season with salt and pepper. Mix together roughly.

3 Place the mushrooms, cap sides down, on a baking sheet and divide the garlic mixture between them. Bake for 35 minutes, then serve with lemon wedges and the truffle aioli.

PER SERVING: ENERGY 590KCAL/2437KJ | PROTEIN 8.2G | CARBOHYDRATE 13.1G, OF WHICH SUGARS 1.6G | FAT 56.5G, OF WHICH SATURATES 16.7G | CHOLESTEROL 205MG | CALCIUM 114MG | FIBRE 4.8G | SODIUM 308MG.

Nutty and sweet, chestnut mushrooms belong with cheese, so why not use this match made in heaven by making chestnut mushrooms into biscuits for cheese? This is a great moist biscuit that could even pass as a sweet biscuit, at a push. Using your hands to shape, the biscuits are easy yet satisfying to make. Eat the fruits of your labour with some ripe Stilton or mature Cheddar – no need for butter.

Chestnut mushroom and oat biscuits

Makes 12
Ready in 30 minutes

- 150g/5oz chestnut mushrooms
- 60g/2½oz/5 tbsp butter, plus extra for greasing
- 150g/5oz rolled oats
- 60g/2¼oz/generous ½ cup wholemeal (whole-wheat) flour, plus extra for dusting
- 2.5g/½ tsp bicarbonate of soda (baking soda)
- 2.5g/½ tsp sugar
- 30ml/2 tbsp crème fraîche
- Pinch sea salt and 5g/1 tsp ground black pepper

1 Preheat the oven to 190°C/375°F/Gas 5 and grease two large baking sheets. In a food processor, blend the mushrooms until very finely chopped. Add the butter and blend for 30 seconds. In a large bowl, combine the oats, flour, bicarbonate of soda and sugar, and season with a pinch of salt and 5g/1 tsp of ground black pepper.

2 Mix the mushroom mixture into the dry ingredients, along with the crème fraîche. Dust a clean surface with flour and roll the mixture into 12 small balls. Press down the balls and shape into circular, flat biscuits, using more flour if they become sticky.

3 Place spaced out on the prepared baking sheets, then bake for 10–15 minutes, until slightly golden and firm. Allow to cool and serve or keep in a sealed container for up to a week.

PER BISCUIT: ENERGY 114KCAL/477KJ | PROTEIN 2.5G | CARBOHYDRATE 12.4G, OF WHICH SUGARS 0.2G | FAT 6.4G, OF WHICH SATURATES 3.3G | CHOLESTEROL 13MG | CALCIUM 12MG | FIBRE 1.9G | SODIUM 606MG.

Based on the age-old French recipe poule au pot, this warming winter dish is usually filled with a breadcrumb stuffing, but we thought mushrooms would be a better idea (well, of course we did). The meaty shiitake, pied bleu, pied de mouton and feathery maitake fill the chicken well, poaching alongside it in its juices and a rich stock of red wine, herbs and orange. To make this exact recipe, you have to get your spindly pied de mouton in time – just before the end of February, depending where you are – but you can simply replace with flat mushrooms after that. The other mushrooms used are grown all year long, so won't be as tricky to find.

Chicken in a pot

Serves 4–6
Ready in 2 hours 25 minutes

- 1 whole chicken
- 100g/3¾oz shallots, peeled and finely chopped
- 150g/5oz baby leeks, trimmed and roughly sliced
- 4 sprigs of rosemary
- 500ml/17fl oz/generous 2 cups mushroom stock (see page 228)
- 10g/2 tsp honey
- 500ml/17fl oz/generous 2 cups red wine
- 400g/14oz mixed shiitake, pied bleu and pied de mouton
- 1 punnet of maitake/hen of the woods, trimmed and broken up slightly
- 3 garlic cloves, crushed
- Juice of 1 orange, plus extra quarters for garnish
- 60g/4 tbsp fresh flat leaf parsley
- 30g/2 tbsp cornflour (cornstarch), mixed in a small pot with 15ml/1 tbsp cold water
- Salt and ground black pepper

1 Take the chicken out of the refrigerator to bring up to room temperature, then in a very large pot, place the shallots, leeks, 2 sprigs of the rosemary, stock, honey and wine. Bring to the boil and season with salt and pepper. Simmer for 10 minutes.

2 In a large bowl, combine all of the mushrooms with the garlic and orange juice. Stuff the bird with the mushroom mixture, along with the remaining 2 sprigs rosemary and half of the parsley, packing it full and securing the stuffing inside by tying the feet up with kitchen string.

3 Put the chicken into the pot and simmer, covered, for 2 hours, stirring in the cornflour paste and the remaining parsley 2 minutes before the end of cooking. Serve immediately, garnished with the extra orange quarters.

PER SERVING: ENERGY 394KCAL/1640KJ | PROTEIN 29.9G | CARBOHYDRATE 9.3G, OF WHICH SUGARS 3.9G | FAT 20.3G, OF WHICH SATURATES 5.6G | CHOLESTEROL 143MG | CALCIUM 34MG | FIBRE 2.9G | SODIUM 114MG.

The pied de mouton mushroom is a sturdy fellow and a great addition to any stew. Soaking up its surrounding flavours, yet still keeping its umami taste and bulky stature, the little 'mutton's foot' can hold its own with the biggest of flavours. So we thought teaming it up with its namesake just for one recipe was too cute an opportunity to miss. We've also added some yellow chanterelles to make it pretty and a whole host of different types of beans to fill you up on a cold winter's day.

Mutton chop and pied de mouton stew

Serves 4
Ready in 55 minutes

- 4 mutton or lamb chops (the flavours suit mutton though)
- 40g/1½oz/3¼ tbsp butter
- 15ml/1 tbsp rapeseed oil
- 15g/1 tbsp rapeseeds
- 5 shallots, halved
- 4 baby turnips, halved
- 5g/1 tsp honey
- 2 garlic cloves, sliced
- 200g/7oz pied de mouton
- 400g/14oz canned borlotti beans, drained and rinsed
- 400g/14oz canned haricot (navy) beans, drained and rinsed
- 400g/14oz canned cannellini or butter beans, drained and rinsed
- 300ml/½ pint/1¼ cups white wine
- 450ml/¾ pint/scant 2 cups chicken stock
- 15g/1 tbsp thyme leaves
- 200g/7oz yellow chanterelles
- 1 Little Gem (Bibb) lettuce, sliced
- Salt and ground white pepper
- Crusty bread, to serve
- Fresh mint sprigs, for garnish

1 On a plate, season the mutton chops with salt and white pepper and set aside. In a large casserole dish, melt 20g/¾oz/1½ tbsp of the butter. Add the oil and stir in the rapeseeds. Cook the mutton chops in the butter, oil and rapeseeds, sealing for 3 minutes on each side. Transfer to a plate with a slotted spoon and cover with foil.

2 Add the shallots and turnips to the casserole dish and sauté for 5 minutes, then mix in the honey, garlic and pied de mouton, sautéing for a further minute. Mix in all of the beans and the white wine and simmer for 5 minutes, then add the chicken stock and thyme and bring to the boil.

3 Return mutton chops to the casserole and simmer, with the lid on, for 25 minutes, adding the chanterelles 5 minutes before the end of cooking. Stir in the lettuce and remaining butter, and serve with crusty bread, garnished with mint.

PER SERVING: ENERGY 491KCAL/2053KJ | PROTEIN 36G | CARBOHYDRATE 29.8G, OF WHICH SUGARS 7G | FAT 20.8G, OF WHICH SATURATES 9.4G | CHOLESTEROL 95MG | CALCIUM 85MG | FIBRE 14.3G | SODIUM 890MG.

The king of the forest, ceps are the ultimate treat on toast and the mushroom wholesaler's favourite snack in season. And if the weather is mild and the season's on your side, you can still get South African ceps at Christmas time. A much-prized Christmas Day appetizer in Michael's household, these meaty, creamy mushrooms are a dream with some sweet sherry, to bring out their natural sugars and a large slice of bread to mop up all the rich juices.

Ceps on toast or the wholesaler's snack

Serves 2
Ready in 10 minutes

- 15ml/1 tbsp rapeseed oil
- 1 garlic clove, crushed
- 150g/5oz ceps, sliced
- 30ml/2 tbsp sherry
- Zest and juice of 1 lemon
- 15g/1 tbsp chopped fresh flat leaf parsley
- 2 slices of sourdough or granary bread
- Sea salt and black pepper
- Grated Parmesan cheese, for garnish

1 In a large frying pan, heat the oil, then sauté the garlic for 1 minute. Add the mushrooms and fry until golden, then add the sherry, cooking for 1 minute, until reduced.

2 Stir in the lemon zest and juice, then the parsley, and season. Serve on top of the bread, toasted if you like, or along with crusty bread. Serve, garnished with Parmesan.

PER SERVING: ENERGY 150KCAL/629KJ | PROTEIN 4.5G | CARBOHYDRATE 15G, OF WHICH SUGARS 1.4G | FAT 6.7G, OF WHICH SATURATES 0.6G | CHOLESTEROL 0MG | CALCIUM 83MG | FIBRE 3.2G | SODIUM 171MG.

Using an array of beautiful Asian-original cultivated mushrooms, this broth is easy to make, tasty and textured to eat and good for you. Mushrooms have long been an important part of Chinese medicine and this soup is packed full of vitamins and minerals to ward off a cold. It's also a feel-good eating experience, with lots of different textures from the thick, velvety black fungus to the pop of the oval straw mushrooms, flavoured with warming garlic, ginger and coriander.

Chinese broth

Serves 6–8
Ready in 20 minutes

- 5ml/1 tsp vegetable oil
- 2 garlic cloves, crushed
- 5cm/2in piece of root ginger, thinly sliced
- 5g/1 tsp ground coriander
- 1.5 litres/2½ pints/6¼ cups vegetable stock
- 15ml/1 tbsp chinkiang vinegar
- 25g/1oz dried black fungus, soaked and drained, retaining the liquid, sliced
- 1 x can straw mushrooms, rinsed and drained
- 100g/3¾oz oyster mushrooms
- 2 eryngii, sliced
- 1 packet enoki
- 1 packet white shimeji
- 1 packet of nori sheets, cut into strips (optional)
- 1 pak choi (bok choy) or any green cabbage, pulled apart and roughly chopped
- Soy sauce, to serve

1 Heat the oil in a large pan and add the garlic, ginger and coriander, and stir fry for 2 minutes. Add the vegetable stock and vinegar, as well as the reserved black fungus soaking liquid. Bring to the boil.

2 Add all of the mushrooms and simmer, covered, for 15 minutes. Mix in the nori, if using, and pak choi or cabbage, and serve, with soy sauce to taste.

PER SERVING: ENERGY 29KCAL/122KJ | PROTEIN 3.2G | CARBOHYDRATE 1.1G, OF WHICH SUGARS 0.8G | FAT 1.4G, OF WHICH SATURATES 0.2G | CHOLESTEROL 0MG | CALCIUM 61MG | FIBRE 2.7G | SODIUM 155MG.

THE MUSHROOM MAN

Michael Hyams is based in the famous New Covent Garden Market in London, operating under his popular company name of Mushroom Man, and supplying both wild and cultivated mushrooms to chefs and the restaurant industry. He offers all the wild and cultivated essentials at the right time in the season, as well as promoting new or new-to-market varieties by popping them into mushroom box mixes – a great way to introduce different varieties to chefs. Michael provides films, adverts and a range of commercial photography with edible fungi in his ongoing crusade to promote mushrooms.

Michael's family goes back several generations within the wholesale Covent Garden Market, which has moved from Covent Garden to Vauxhall in that time. Michael's granddad, father and quite a few cousins and relatives worked in the original Covent Garden. His granddad worked in the fruit and veg market, whilst his grandma cooked in the very famous pub, The Coach and Horses on Wellington Street.

His father started as a junior salesperson on the fruit side of his cousin's business and as a little boy, it caught Michael's imagination – boxes on shoulders, and market banter. When Michael was 13, his dad thought it was a good idea for him to get a Saturday and holiday job. It was hard work, packing the stall over and over again, over long hours, but he loved it. By 22, Michael was running his own busy vegetable retail stall near the family home, at a time when street markets were one of the few options to buy fresh produce. As the stall started to sell to the odd café in Kingston, Michael realized that the real buzz was in selling to restaurants – and that there was no better place to do that than the West End.

Michael started supplying to Zanzibar's chef Alastair Little and top independent chef Rowley Leigh in the mid-70s, and built his business from there, going on to serve the Roux Brothers and Nico Ladenis. He learnt what chefs really wanted and how to deliver that at the very dawn of the British chef revolution – a big opportunity. The Soho restaurant scene was getting exciting; in those days you could park your van and spend time talking and exchanging ideas, with all the produce coming from the food hub that was Covent Garden. In 1974 the market moved to a small unit in Vauxhall, and in 2003 Michael (with his colleague, the late Phil Dean) moved to the New Covent Garden Market and Mushroom Man was born.

The timing of the move to the new wholesale market was spot on – surrounded as they were by chef's suppliers and coming face-to-face with the buyers, in a period when London chefs were making a new name for themselves. Mushroom Man has grown organically, offering quality, provenance, traceability and reliability, and was probably the first company that stocked the full range from the button to the morel.

Michael's love of food is longstanding. He makes a point of eating in newly opened venues every week and has visited as many of the restaurants his mushrooms have ended up in as he can. From visiting the farms and forests that produce the mushrooms he trades in, to eating the mushrooms at the end of the food chain, Michael finds a joy in it all.

LIZ O'KEEFE met Michael and discovered his 'mushroom grotto' in her first job in food journalism more than a decade ago at the trade publication Fresh Produce Journal, which at the time was based in the New Covent Garden Market. Having gone into kitchens at 15 years old, she qualified as a chef whilst doing her A levels, working her way up to chef de partie during her English degree. Over the five years she wrote for FPJ, travelling all over the UK and the world reporting on fresh produce, Liz would always come back to Mushroom Man to see what was new and 'borrow' boxes of different mushrooms to experiment with, especially when she moved on to become cookery editor of monthly foodie magazine, *Eat In*. In the meantime, Liz set Mushroom Man up on Twitter – whether Michael liked it or not – and continued to foster a following for the supplier of all these weird and wonderful mushrooms.

Now a freelance food writer, recipe developer, supper club host and food stylist, Liz believes that people only really appreciate cooking and eating when they know about how their food has got to them. Never too far away from mushrooms, from her earliest foraging expeditions as a child to today, Liz works alongside Michael and Mushroom Man, with a mission to let everyone know just how good mushrooms are.

INDEX

ACKNOWLEDGEMENTS

This edition is published by Lorenz Books
an imprint of Anness Publishing Ltd
info@anness.com
www.lorenzbooks.com
www.annesspublishing.com

If you like the images in this book and would like to investigate using them for publishing, promotions or advertising, please visit our website www.practicalpictures.com for more information.

A CIP catalogue record for this book is available from the British Library.

Publisher: Joanna Lorenz
Photography: Jon Ashford
Prop styling: Jon Ashford & Pene Parker
Recipes and food styling: Liz O'Keefe
Food styling assistant: Natalie Pavich
Designer: Pene Parker
Illustrations: Georgie Fearns
Editorial: Sarah Lumby
Mycological consultant: Clifford Davy

PUBLISHER'S NOTE
Although the advice and information in this book are believed to be accurate and true at the time of going to press, neither the authors nor the publisher can accept any legal responsibility or liability for any errors or omissions that may have been made nor for any inaccuracies nor for any loss, harm or injury that comes about from following instructions or advice in this book.

The publishers and the authors cannot accept responsibility for any identification of any mushroom made by the users of this guide. Although many species are edible for many people, some species cause allergic reactions or illness to some people. Therefore, the publishers and authors cannot take responsibility for any effects resulting from eating any mushroom.

COOK'S NOTES
Bracketed terms are intended for American readers.

For all recipes, quantities are given in both metric and imperial measures and, where appropriate, in standard cups and spoons. Follow one set of measures, but not a mixture, because they are not interchangeable.

Standard spoon and cup measures are level. 1 tsp = 5ml, 1 tbsp = 15ml, 1 cup = 250ml/8fl oz.

Australian standard tablespoons are 20ml. Australian readers should use 3 tsp in place of 1 tbsp for measuring small quantities.

American pints are 16fl oz/2 cups. American readers should use 20fl oz/2.5 cups in place of 1 pint when measuring liquids.

Electric oven temperatures in this book are for conventional ovens. When using a fan oven, the temperature will probably need to be reduced by about 10–20°C/20–40°F. Since ovens vary, you should check with your manufacturer's instruction book for guidance.

The nutritional analysis given for each recipe is calculated per portion (i.e. serving or item), unless otherwise stated. If the recipe gives a range, such as Serves 4–6, then the nutritional analysis will be for the smaller portion size, i.e. 6 servings. The analysis does not include optional ingredients, such as salt added to taste.

Medium (US large) eggs are used unless otherwise stated.